"AS MANY AS
I LOVE …"

Published by CFI Book Division
P.O. Box 159, Gordonsville, Tennessee 38563

ISBN: 979-8-9868765-8-0

Contents

Foreword 9

1. We Must Listen to What Christ Is Saying! 11

2. Is Christ Welcome in Laodicea? 19

3. What Is Special About
    A Day-Of-Atonement Repentance? 26

4. How A Deeper Repentance
    Pervades The "Body" 37

5. Christ's Repentance For Sins He Never Committed 43

6. How Christ Called the Ancient Jews to
    National Repentance 53

7. Ancient Israel's Full Cup of Impenitence 60

8. Christ's Call To The Remnant
    Church To Repent 66

9. How Can A Church Of Millions
    Of Members Repent? 76

10. What Our Denominational History Tells Us 83

11. Bible Repentance: Path to Christlike Love 94

Appendix A
    A Repentance of Ministers And Their Families 103

Appendix B
    Laodicea Is Not Doomed 105

Appendix C
    Ezekiel 18 and Corporate Guilt 109

"As many as I love,
I rebuke and chasten:
be zealous therefore,
and repent."
(Revelation 3:19)

"AS MANY AS I LOVE ..."

CHRIST'S CALL
TO LAODICEA

By ROBERT J. WIELAND

Foreword

In this day Seventh-day Adventists live with the hope that soon there will appear in the east that "small … cloud … the sign of the Son of man." Blessed day! What rejoicing! But—can that day come so long as God's people consider the time of the second coming of Christ to be solely His responsibility? Is this fair to God? Has He no right to expect more from His people than spiritual self-seeking?

This small book deals with the basic problem of heart-motivation. It searches the recesses of the Adventist conscience. It stresses the final call of the True Witness. After 6000 years of waiting to see the conquest of sin, the Saviour makes His last plea. This has gone unheeded for well over a century. There is no further call!

The truth which is to test the world in the end-time has not yet been understood, appreciated, nor have God's chosen people really been tested by it. How long can the remnant church continue with "business-as-usual?" What will banish the misconceptions so prevalent in our midst today?

There is more than a small group in the church who say that persecution must do the necessary work. It alone will drive out wrong ideas. But what are we doing now or planning to do in the near future which will bring persecution? Is persecution the cause or the effect of God's people being absolutely committed to His call? How does persecution fit into the day-of-atonement which Adventists have long held as vital to the final ministry of the True Witness? And then, if it is the enemy of God who presses for persecution, why is he waiting and what will eventually trigger this trying time?

We are not the first people to have misunderstood the message God sent. The ancient Jews brought grief and sorrow to the Messiah because they were certain they understood—but they didn't. His unheeded call to Old Jerusalem to repent could hardly have brought more heartbreak to the Saviour than the lukewarm, unknowing response He receives from the last of the seven churches today. The Jews were waiting for the Son of David to take the throne and rule in splendor. Their national rejection of the Saviour must surely run parallel with our insistence that He remain outside the door knocking for admission.

Our house will be left unto us "desolate" if we forget the persistent assurance by Christ that He will return. Therefore the history of our spiritual forefathers demands careful study and clear understanding. It is possible that this book can bring to the remnant church the key to unlock our denominational failures and illuminate the way to spiritual victory.

How could the God of the universe do more than He has done to make His personal plea to His "angel of the church of the Laodiceans?" But the truth is, he has done more! He offers everything needed to change a wretched, miserable, poor, blind and naked Laodicea into a believing, properly clothed, discerning remnant church—humbly repentant and overcoming even as He overcame.

May the Lord use the message of this book to bring Seventh-day Adventists to understand and receive the call of the True Witness. Responding to this heavenly call will bring the repentance of the ages so that the High Priest will be able to rise up and proclaim, "It is done." The power of the gospel will have proved its strength, the atonement will be demonstrated to be complete.

Donald K. Short

Chapter 1

We Must Listen to What Christ Is Saying!

Our sinful, despairing modern world desperately needs a Spirit-filled Seventh-day Adventist Church. We begin with a deep conviction: this church is the prophetic "remnant" of Revelation 12:17, a unique people with whom the dragon is "wroth" and makes "war" because they are called to "keep the commandments of God, and have the testimony of Jesus." This same group tell the world the true good news of "the everlasting gospel" (ch. 14:6-12). They are a vital ingredient in world stability.

Although this sense of destiny has kept the Seventh-day Adventist Church on course for over a century, it leaves us no room for pride. Another message in Revelation is very unflattering. Christ's direct rebuke "to the angel of the church of the Laodiceans" applies specifically to us.

The Lord says that we are "lukewarm, … wretched, and miserable, and poor, and blind, and naked" (Revelation 3:14-17). The original language implies that our pathetic condition is outstanding and spectacular among all the "seven churches" of history.

Countless sermons have been preached and articles published about this message. But we today generally recognize that it still applies. The average Adventist congregation of a century ago could not have been any more lukewarm than most of our churches are today.

Therefore it makes sense to ask, "Have we done what the Faithful and True Witness says?" The passing decades compel us to wrestle with serious questions. If time must go on and on, will there be a Seventh-day Adventist church a hundred years from now as lukewarm as ours is today?

If we have successfully overcome these spiritual weaknesses, there should by now be some clear evidence as to how and when the overcoming took place. Reason dictates that when the church truly overcomes, Christ's coming can no longer be delayed. This is confirmed by His parable about the farmer (Jesus Himself) in Mark 4: "When the fruit is brought forth, immediately he putteth in the sickle, because the harvest is come" (verse 29). The "harvest" is "the end of the world," the second coming (Matthew 13:39; Revelation 14:14-16).

Why hasn't Christ's appeal to His people done its work? When will He have a remnant church that has bought His "gold tried in the fire," His "white raiment," and His "eyesalve"? Or will this never be?

Must we assume that Christ's message will fail in the end? Could He have expected all along that our twentieth century would witness its final defeat? Because ancient Israel failed repeatedly, must modern Israel fail also?

Surely there must be some better news than this! We are living in the time for a victory that never before has taken place in history. We have been assured: "The Holy Spirit is to animate and purify the whole church, purifying and cementing hearts. ... It is the purpose of God to glorify Himself in His people before the world" (*Testimonies*, Vol. 9, p. 20). As surely as the Seventh-day Adventist Church is that "remnant" in Revelation, so surely must this message from Jesus succeed at last.

A Reason That Makes Sense of the Long Delay

As we re-read the words of the True Witness, we come upon a clue as to why the message has not yet finished its work. This is found in the only direct command given in the message: "Whoever is dear to me I reprove and chastise. Be earnest about it, therefore. Repent" (verse 19, NAB). Until that command to repent is obeyed, nothing effective can be done about "buying" the gold, white raiment, and eyesalve. This failure to repent is the hurdle which deserves the focus of our attention.

During all these many decades since the 1850's when we as a people first understood that the message applied to us, it has been assumed that the repentance Christ calls for is only personal and individual. Millions of church members have listened to pulpit and camp meeting appeals to repent, and four or five generations of them have already gone to their graves. They were dedicated people! We must assume that in general they experienced individual repentance before they died, otherwise they would be lost. We cannot imagine that these, our dear forefather-saints, died unrepentant. Surely they died sufficiently repentant to assure them a place in the first resurrection. Is this what Christ means when He says, "Repent"?

If so, "we" have already done our part. If the Lord's call to repent has already accomplished its purpose during our hundred-year-plus history, then the long delay in the coming of Christ must be His fault. But to believe this would create a terrible problem. It would leave us no hope for the future except to continue repeating the history of the past. But if we lose our faith in the nearness of the second coming, we lose the reason for our existence as a special church. There is a close relationship between understanding Christ's Laodicean call to repent and our confidence in the nearness of His coming. This will be clear as we proceed.

The Spiritual Crisis of the Seventh-day Adventist Church

If what Jesus calls for is merely the individual, personal repentance that several generations of Seventh-day Adventists have already experienced, Adventist despair is sure to set in. Christ's coming will recede further into the shadows of our uncertainty. This is one reason why we lose over 65% of our youth after they reach 18. For many, the idea of the Lord's soon return has already lost much significant meaning.

Roland Hegstad, for 26 years editor of *Liberty*, says that Adventism is "not attracting our own youth because all we're doing is asking them to come play church with us" (*Adventist Review*, February 27, 1986). Christ's Laodicean message presents to them no spiritual challenge, for if we have already repented, we must by now be "rich and increased with goods, and have need of nothing" except to carry on business as usual like the world does until the Lord arbitrarily decides He is ready to come the second time. Many have no vital hope that His coming will be in their lifetime.

Can we have a reasonable hope that we will see the Lord's return? Did He deceive our pioneers by telling them it was "near" when all along He knew it would be delayed at least 140 years and no one knows how many more? Is the Calvinist idea true, that the sovereign Lord has predetermined the time of Jesus' second coming whether or not His people will be ready? If so, there is nothing we can do but await the fixed signal in God's predetermined time clock.

But this raises very serious problems. It involves the Lord Himself in an ethical difficulty, for He has often told us through the Spirit of Prophecy that the end is "near." His messenger frequently said things like this: "I saw ... that time can last but very little longer" (*Early Writings*, p. 58; 1850). "Only a moment of time, as it were, yet remains." "The battle of Armageddon is soon to be fought" (*Testimonies*, Vol. 6, pp. 14, 406; 1900). If such warnings of the nearness of the end were merely a "wolf, wolf" cry, the Lord has not been fair with us. For Him repeatedly to say "near" when He didn't mean it or intended a definition of the word foreign to all human comprehension, wouldn't it be unethical for Him to treat His people this way?[1]

If We Lose Our Adventism, We Lose Everything

Further, if we say or feel that our Lord has delayed His coming, we put ourselves in the company of the "evil servant" in the parable who says that very thing (Matthew 24:48). That would destroy any meaningful Adventism. This is because no people can be reconciled to God in a final atonement if they feel that He has deceived them or that their comprehension of His truth has been patently false from their very beginning. This could be the basic problem which underlies much present apostasy and backsliding. There is a deep Adventist spiritual alienation because it appears that inspired messages have been crying "wolf, wolf."

But Scripture makes clear that while God is indeed sovereign, He has chosen to make the actual timing of Christ's second coming dependent on the preparation of His living people. The dead are all hopeless prisoners in the grave, awaiting release at the resurrection whenever that may be. But the living may delay or "hasten on" that day of the second coming of Christ (2 Peter 3:12, NEB, NAS, NIV, NKJV, etc).

In His parable Jesus represents Himself as already eager to return, waiting only until "the fruit is brought forth," whereupon "immediately he putteth in the sickle, because the harvest is ripe" (Mark 4:29). In the Revelation preview of the second coming, an angel tells Him, "The time is come for thee to reap; for the harvest of the earth is ripe" (Revelation 14:15). The long-delayed "marriage of the Lamb" comes quickly once "his bride hath made herself ready" (Revelation 19:7). The repentance Christ calls for is related to the Bride making herself "ready."

> It is the privilege of every Christian not only to look for but to hasten the coming of our Lord Jesus Christ. Were all who profess His name bearing fruit to His glory, how quickly the whole world would be sown with the seed of the gospel. Quickly the last great harvest would be ripened, and Christ would come to gather the precious grain. (*Christ's Object Lessons*, p. 69).

To go on being lukewarm and dying, generation after generation, cannot be a proper response of a Bride to Christ's last-church appeal.

A Deeper Meaning in Christ's Call to Repent

It is obvious that the Laodicean repentance Christ calls for has never yet taken place. But this very fact gives us hope, for there is something that our faith can rectify. Zechariah tells of a repentance that will grip the hearts of "the house of David" and "the inhabitants of Jerusalem," making possible in them a cleansing work so Christ can return (Zechariah 12:10-13:1).

The promise to Laodicea of a seat upon Christ's throne is the most exalted in Scripture. But the message itself is not addressed to individuals as such, but "unto the angel of the church of the Laodiceans," or in Zechariah's phrase, "the house of David" and "the inhabitants of Jerusalem." This is the corporate body of the church and its leadership. Christ's final promise is directed to the same personified body, not merely to individuals: "To him that overcometh [the angel of the church of the Laodiceans] will I grant to sit with me in my throne, even as I also overcame, and am set down with my Father in his throne" (Revelation 3:21).

This ultimate honor will be accorded to a generation, a body of God's people who will respond to His appeal, "Repent!" It cannot refer merely to certain individuals who personally repent, irrespective of "the angel of the church." Confusion on this point has fueled the fanatical idea that individuals must leave Laodicea and return to Philadelphia, which would set the clock back more than a century and put the final events into reverse gear. Nowhere does Christ call individuals to leave Laodicea; He calls on "the angel of the church" to repent.[2]

A probe into the meaning of repentance is not "negative." Rather, feeling satisfied with the status quo is the really negative attitude, because such spiritual laissez faire indefinitely postpones the return of Christ. Many in the church hunger and thirst for a clearer grasp of vital truth for these last days. They know that the coming of the Lord has been long delayed and that we, not Heaven, are responsible. They sense that pinpointing the reason for repentance and exploring how to experience it is the most "positive" course we can pursue. Repentance by "the body" does not deny or displace personal, individual repentance. Rather, we will see how it deepens it and makes it effective. Such repentance can alone meet the needs of Laodicea in the final Day of Atonement. The daily ministry in the first apartment of the Levitical sanctuary took care of individuals' needs; the annual Day of Atonement was concerned about the need of Israel as a congregation.

All repentance is personal and individual. But "as the body [the church] is one, and hath many members, and all the members of that one body, being many, are one body" (1 Corinthians 12:12), so we bear a relationship to the Head and to one another that can only be expressed in the word corporate. The word has nothing to do with committees or conferences or segments of church hierarchical organization. It means "relating to the body" and to its Head.

Christ's call to "repent" is directed to "the angel of the church of the Laodiceans." No individual can ever be the "bride" of Christ, for as individuals, God's people are all merely "guests" at the wedding. The corporate body of the overcoming church will be the bride. Something has delayed her getting "ready." It is a deeper layer of sin that He says, "Thou knowest not" (Revelation 3:17). It makes sense to realize that the repentance which that deeper sin requires must itself also be deeper. However disturbing, the Lord's call must be faced honestly.

Repentance is both sorrow for sin and turning away from it. But repentance can be only superficial if our understanding of the sin itself is superficial. We readily quote the text that says, "If we confess our sins, he [Christ] is faithful and just to forgive us our sins, and to cleanse us from all unrighteousness" (1 John 1:9). But the context of this promise does not encourage a superficial assurance that the tape recording of our sins is scrubbed by pressing a magic button. John is emphasizing how easily "we deceive ourselves" so that "the truth is not in us" while we remain in this Laodicean state of lukewarmness. So long as Jesus' pathetic diagnosis that "thou knowest not" remains valid, so long do "we deceive ourselves." We cannot be truly cleansed from deep sin that we do not understandably "confess" (See 1 John 1:8, 10).

The message to Laodicea is not child's play. "One like unto the Son of man" with "eyes as a flame of fire" and "his voice as the sound of many waters" is calling His people to the most profound experience of the ages. Failure to recognize that He calls us to corporate and denominational repentance creates confusion and apostasy, and is an eventual time-bomb of self-destruction.

Our Lord says, "As many as I love, I rebuke and chasten." But let us not resist His appeal because our natural hearts tend to resent His rebuke. It's the clearest evidence we have of His love! To resist it is to resist our only hope.

"He that hath an ear, let him hear what the Spirit saith unto the churches," especially the last one.

---

1. New Testament evidence indicates that Christ and His apostles did not teach the early church to expect the second coming in their generation. 2 Thessalonians

2:1-10 makes clear that the apostles had at least a rudimentary comprehension of the time sweep of Daniel's prophecies. Likewise, the statement, "Behold, I come quickly" in Revelation has always been understood as applying in a proleptic sense to those living in the end of time. Surely, God has not deceived His people for 2000 years, nor have they thought so!

2. See Appendix B concerning the Philadelphia-Laodicea relationship.

Chapter 2

Is Christ Welcome in Laodicea?

Human sin blossomed out into the murder of the Son of God. Those who crucified Him the first time were forgiven, for Jesus prayed for them, "They know not what they do" (Luke 23:34).

Sincere as we are, could we repeat their sin, again not knowing what we do? There are those who "crucify to themselves the Son of God afresh, and put him to an open shame" (Hebrews 6:6). Is Laodicea's sin related to this? How deep is the sin for which "the angel of the church of the Laodiceans" must repent?

Laodicea shares something in common with Israel of old—an ignorance of our true state. The Lord says, "You ... do not know," the same as He prayed of them, "They know not." This means that the remnant church is pathetically unaware of her actual role as she appears on the stage of the universe. "You are ... naked," Christ whispers to us in warning (Revelation 3:17, NKJV). Could this be more serious than we have thought, more than mere shameful naivete? Could it stem from a deep heart alienation from the Lord Himself, something that makes us akin to the ancient Jews?

The idea of nakedness surfaces again in the parable of the wedding garment. The deluded guest who thought that dressing up was optional was not only stupid. He lacked respect for the host. An alienation deeper than his conscious understanding poisoned his feelings toward his host (Matthew 22:11-13). The "final atonement" must bring the solution to this alienation—a very serious problem." The carnal mind is enmity against God," says Paul; and enmity will always blossom into murder if it runs its course, for "whosoever hateth his brother is a murderer," says

John (Romans 8:7; 1 John 3:15). Seventh-day Adventists are friends of Jesus and so would not knowingly crucify Him afresh. But being His friends doesn't necessarily guarantee that we will treat Him right, for we read that He was once "wounded in the house of [His] friends" (Zechariah 13:6). But has He been wounded more than once?

Many statements from the Lord's messenger declare that the same enmity against Christ that characterized the ancient Jews has been manifested in Seventh-day Adventist history. Further, this inspired writer says that this "just-like-the-Jews" spirit has been the root of our basic spiritual problem for most of a century.

It is easy to suppose that Laodicea, being lukewarm, is not very bad and not very good. Her sin must be a mild one. We have often acted and spoken as though Heaven is quite proud of us. Could it really be true that Christ is being crucified afresh in Laodicea?

Our spiritual knowledge has not kept pace with the tremendous increase of scientific knowledge in the world. No one of us in this computer age would want to live in a cave and count on an abacus by candlelight. But spiritually speaking, Christ represents His last-day church as virtually poverty stricken. We are a pathetic sight to Heaven. We shall someday look back on our era as the dark ages. Jesus must be sorry that He still needs to say of us, "The children of this world are in their generation wiser than the children of light" (Luke 16:8). In an age of exploding knowledge in technology, God's people have not broken through this spiritual barrier of "thou knowest-not." The last unexplored continent is not Antarctica, but the inner depths of Laodicea's soul. The enmity therein, Christ says, "Thou knowest not."

The Cross and the Pathology of Sin

Modern science has discovered that harmful bacteria and viruses produce disease. While pathology identifies these tiny enemy organisms, our understanding of what sin is and how it proliferates has not kept pace with the world's knowledge of how disease works.

Yet we are near the time when Christ's intercession as High Priest must end. If any alienation from God or enmity against Him survives beneath the surface at that time, this spiritual virus will develop unchecked. Armageddon will be the result—full scale, uninhibited warfare against Christ without the restraint now imposed by the Holy Spirit. In essence, all sin is a re-crucifixion of Christ, and its final display will be Armageddon. We need a better understanding of the nature and depth of sin, and what is the science of salvation from it. No one can deny that sin has abounded in our modern age; knowledge of more abounding grace is essential now.

The master inventor of all fiendish schemes has vowed eternal enmity against Laodicea, "to make war with the remnant ... which keep the commandments of God and have the testimony of Jesus Christ" (Revelation 12:17). He wants to embarrass Christ. This is his best way to sabotage His kingdom. If Satan can perpetuate sin among God's people, he has his success made. Let's face a realistic fact: continued lukewarmness now is sin. And as time goes on, it will be seen to be a re-crucifixion of Christ.

The enemy cannot at present use physical force. His strategy has been to take advantage of our ignorance of what sin is and thus induce in us a kind of spiritual paralysis. Our phenomenal lukewarmness is an enchanted-ground lethargy on the borders of heaven.

But what is the pathology of lukewarmness? How do succeeding generations of Adventists get re-infected by it? How does it spread even to Third World churches? It must be caused by a sin virus. If so, what is the nature of that sin? Why haven't we found healing for it? As we proceed, answers will become apparent.

In Christ's special appeal to us to repent, we meet the challenge of the ages. Peter's sermon at Pentecost unlocks our understanding of it. He shocked the listening Jews with the news that latent enmity against God had flared out in the crucifixion of their Messiah. The Holy Spirit used his sermon to press home to their hearts the conviction of how awful that sin was. They cried out, "What shall we do?"

The apostle's answer was, "Repent" (Acts 2:22-38). And they responded! They received the Holy Spirit in a measure that has never since been equalled. But it will be surpassed in that final reception of the Holy Spirit known as the latter rain. But something has held it up for many decades.

Not only are we frustrated by the long delay; Christ Himself is deeply disappointed. The agony of a suffering, terrorized world weighs heavily upon Him. He cannot take a vacation to some remote corner of His universe and forget it. In our weakness, we can feel a little for the agonies of starving, homeless, despairing people when we know about them, yet Jesus is infinitely more sensitive and compassionate than the best of us. "In all their affliction He was afflicted," in ancient times (Isaiah 63:9), and He is still the same today.

> Those who think of the result of hastening or hindering the gospel think of it in relation to themselves and to the world. Few think of its relation to God. Few give thought to the suffering that sin has caused our Creator. All heaven suffered in Christ's agony; but that suffering did not begin or end with His manifestation in humanity. The cross is a revelation to our dull senses of the pain that, from its very inception, sin has brought to the heart of God. Every departure from the right, every deed of cruelty, every failure of humanity to reach His ideal, brings grief to him (*Education*, p. 263).

Our Lord is not an impassive Buddha-like deity in a nirvana trance. Our prayers do not move Him to a pity that He would not otherwise feel. When we beg Him, "Please do something to help," He responds hopefully, "Why don't you do something?" When the mind and heart of "the angel of the church" are truly at-one with Christ, the roadblock will be eliminated and He will employ His people effectively to do what He wants done for the world. Especially of Seventh-day Adventists, we read: "In every church in our land, there is needed confession, repentance, and reconversion. The disappointment of Christ is beyond description" (*Review and Herald*, December 15, 1904). How can we relieve that disappointment?

The Lord's Problem Has Become the Crisis of the Ages

So long as we revel in the comforts of luxurious modern life, we seem not to feel the frustration in the heart of Christ that a century of delay has brought to Him. The Bible reveals God in a dimension unknown in the Qur'an, the Vedic Hindu, or Buddhist scriptures. The world's pain is God's pain, only intensified. Think how a loving, sensitive father feels the pain of a wounded child; then multiply that over four billion times.

Revelation goes a step further and pictures Christ as an eager Bridegroom who longs for "the marriage of the Lamb" to come soon, but He is disappointed that His "bride" has not yet "made herself ready" (Revelation 19:7-9). She has kept Him at arm's length all this while. This means that as yet she can not be truly reconciled to Him. When she is at-one with Him in heart and mind, every church will be pulsating with the life of the Holy Spirit, overflowing with Christlike love. Each will be spiritually alert, radiant with a miraculous unselfishness that transforms each member into a unique revelation of Christ.

Some inspired statements declare that this full-fledged revival will never take in the "whole church," because there will always be tares among the wheat. But there are other equally inspired statements that say that "the whole church" is to be animated and pervaded by the Holy Spirit, overflowing with Christlike love, spiritually alert, radiant with a miraculous unselfishness that transforms each member into a unique revelation of Christ. How can these apparent contradictions be harmonized?

God's purpose in His people will be gloriously fulfilled in "a revival of true godliness among us," "that the way of the Lord may be prepared," "a great movement—a work of revival—going forward in many places. Our people were moving into line, responding to God's call." "The spirit of prayer will actuate every believer and will banish from the church the spirit of discord and strife. ... All will be in harmony with the mind of the Spirit." "In visions of the night, representations passed before me of a great reformatory movement among God's people ... even as was manifested before the day of Pentecost. ... The world seemed to be lightened with the heavenly influence. ...There seemed to be a reformation such as we witnessed in 1844. ... Covetous ones became separated from the company of believers" (cf. *Testimonies*, Vol. 9, pp. 20-23, 46, 47, 126; Vol. 8, pp. 247-251; *Selected Messages*, Book One, pp. 116, 117, 121-128). The apparent contradictions are resolved by the fact that there is a pre-shaking and a post-shaking church; the post-shaken church will fulfill these prophecies. This grand finale of the work of God's Spirit will be a work of extraordinary beauty and simplicity:

Those who wait for the Bridegroom's coming are to say to the people, "Behold your God." The last rays of merciful light, the last message of mercy to be given to the world, is a revelation of His character of love. The children of God are to manifest His glory (*Christ's Object Lessons*, pp. 415, 416).

The good news is that these words will come true! The announcement will yet be sounded, "The marriage of the Lamb is come, and his wife hath made herself ready. And to her was granted that she should be arrayed in fine linen, clean and white: for the fine linen is the righteousness of saints" (Revelation 19:7, 8). The key to fulfillment lies in the repentance that Christ calls for.

How Can This Active and Powerful Love Be Realized?

Executive committee actions, polished programs, high pressure promotion, can never truly motivate. Truth must be the vehicle, reaching human hearts, for only truth can penetrate the secret recesses of Laodicea's soul. The Lord has in reserve a means of motivation that will be fully effective. Something happened at Pentecost which fueled the early church with a phenomenal spiritual energy. It must and will happen again.

That fantastic motivation flowed naturally out of a unique repentance. No sin in all time was more horrendous than that which those people were guilty of—murdering the Son of God. Mankind's deep-seated "enmity against God" had finally produced its full fruitage, (cf. Romans 8:7). But they were only our surrogates, acting on our behalf. By nature, we are no less guilty simply because by accident we were born many centuries later.

Sin has always been "enmity against God," but no one ever fully understood its dimensions until the Holy Spirit drove the truth home to the hearts of Peter's audience that fiftieth day after the resurrection. The realization of their guilt came over them like a flood. Theirs was no petty seeking for security or reward in heaven, nor was it a craven search to evade punishment. The cross of the ages was towering over them, and their human hearts responded to its reality.

A repentance like that of Pentecost is what Christ calls for from us today. It will come, like a lost vein of gold in the earth that must surface again in another place. Our hazy, indistinct idea of repentance can produce only what we see today—hazy, indistinct devotion, lukewarmness. Like medicine taken in quantity sufficient to produce a concentration in the blood stream, our repentance must be comprehensive, full-range, in order for the Holy Spirit to do a fully effective work.

Why Laodicea's Repentance Must Now Be Different in Depth and Extent

This full spectrum of repentance is included in "the everlasting gospel." But its clearest definition has been impossible until now, as history reaches the last of the seven churches. The original word "repentance" means a looking back from the perspective of the end: *metanoia*, from *meta* ("after") and *nous* ("mind"). Thus, repentance can never be complete until the end of history. Like the great Day of Atonement, its full dimension must be a last-day experience. To that moment in time we have now come.

Unless our veiled eyes can see the depth of our sin as identical to that of Peter's congregation at Pentecost, only a veneer repentance can be possible. This in turn can produce only more generations of lukewarm church members, and thus intensify the Lord's problem. Repenting only of superficial sin leaves a deep stratum of further alienation which remains unrealized, unconfessed, and therefore unhealed. It is not enough that sin be legally forgiven; it must also be blotted out. This problem of unrealized sin pervades the entire church in all lands, and its practical effects weaken the witness of every congregation. (Even Third World churches become lukewarm).

Chapter 3

What Is Special About
A Day-Of-Atonement Repentance?

We must understand why there must be a special heavenly Day of Atonement. Involved in it is a special experience for God's people on earth, but this does not imply that God has arbitrarily withheld that unique blessing from previous generations. It would not be fair for Him to grant the last generation something He deliberately kept away from others in past ages.

Previous generations simply did not avail themselves of the full grace that Heaven has always wanted to bestow. The long delay of thousands of years has not been necessary because of God's unwillingness to give, but because of man's unreadiness to receive. The prophetic word, "Unto two thousand three hundred days, then shall the sanctuary be cleansed" (Daniel 8:14), is a prediction that during the last era of human history, God's people will grow into a mature faith that will make possible their full reception of Heaven's grace. The prophecy of Daniel comprehends their spiritual development "unto the measure of the stature of the fulness of Christ" (Ephesians 4:13), not growth on the part of God.

God withheld nothing from Adam that arbitrarily kept him out of the company of the 144,000. His own spiritual immaturity was what kept him from appropriating all the grace that an infinite God would have granted even then. The sanctuary could have been cleansed in ancient times if the historical development of humanity had made it possible. God's infinite resources cannot be limited; the deficiency has been on our side. A final generation will receive the gift of repentance, a *metanoia*, an after-perception that views past history in the light of contrition. Then it can be said, "The marriage of the Lamb has come, and his wife hath made herself ready."

Jesus' call to repent is to every generation, for "all have sinned." "The knowledge of sin" comes through "the law" (Romans 3:23, 20). Thanks to the work of the Holy Spirit, this wholesome knowledge of our guilt is imparted to "every man." It is a "light" that passes by no one (John 1:9).

King David's double crime of adultery and murder illustrates how the Holy Spirit brings conviction of sin. After seducing Bathsheba, he eliminated her husband Uriah. For the Holy Spirit to abandon him would have been the crudest punishment possible. Instead, God still loved him. The Holy Spirit pricked him with sharp conviction. "Day and night thy hand was heavy upon me," David says. The Lord "broke" his "bones," metaphorically. Then, David adds, "I acknowledged my sin unto thee, and mine iniquity have I not hid. I said, I will confess my transgressions unto the Lord; thou forgavest the iniquity of my sin." He begged, "Cast me not away from thy presence; and take not thy holy spirit from me" (Psalm 32:4, 5; 51:8, 11). This was genuine repentance.

One may never have heard the name of Christ, but he senses in his heart that he has "sinned, and come short of the glory of God" (Romans 3:23). There is an awareness, however dim, of a perfect standard in the divine law and in Christ. The Holy Spirit penetrates human hearts with the conviction of "sin, and of righteousness" (John 16:8-10).

Guilt, Like Pain, Is a Signal That Something Is Wrong

The Lord Himself who "so loved the world that He gave His only begotten Son" has prepared the way for His gospel. He has given humanity this capacity to feel the personal pain of conviction of sin. It is a clear evidence of His love!

Legalism or a perverted "gospel" short-circuits this work of the Holy Spirit in human hearts, and as a consequence millions are not able to experience the repentance which alone can heal the hurt they feel deep inside. But Scripture foretells a time when the gospel will be restored to its pristine purity and the earth will be "lightened" with its glory (Revelation 18:1-4). It will be like restoring a broken electric connection. The circuit will be complete—the Holy Spirit's conviction of sin will be complemented by the pure gospel, and the current of heaven's forgiveness will flow through every repentant soul.

A wound in the body causes messages of pain to be relayed to the brain. While a pain-killing drug can superficially alleviate the discomfort, it provides no healing. Serious disease or death can follow an artificial suppression of symptoms. But this is what happens when the sinner rejects the pain of the Holy Spirit's merciful conviction of sin. Pain in the body is a blessing, for it prompts one to seek healing. African lepers, whose sense of pain is anesthetized, actually lose fingers at night, bitten by rats because they can not feel. How much more is it foolish and fatal to fight the Holy Spirit's painful conviction of sin. Repentance is the only proper healing response.

The grateful sinner prays, "Thank You, Lord, for loving me so much as to convict me of my sin. I confess the full truth. You have provided a Substitute who bears my penalty in my stead, and I am motivated by His love to separate from the sin that has crucified Him." This was the miracle that occurred in David's heart when he prayed, "I will declare mine iniquity; I will be sorry for my sin" (Psalm 38:18).

Such repentance is not only sorrow for sin and its results, but a genuine abhorrence of it. It produces an actual turning away from the sin. The law can never do this for anyone; the miracle is administered by grace. "The law worketh wrath," imparting only a terror of judgment, but grace works a repentance that makes "old things" pass away; "behold, all things are become new" (Romans 4:15; 2 Corinthians 5:17). Sin that was once loved is now hated, and righteousness that was once hated is now loved. "The goodness of God leadeth thee to repentance" (Romans 2:4).

This is why repentance includes the actual "remission of sins," that is, sending them away (Luke 24:47). The New Testament word for "forgiveness" implies a separation from sin, a deliverance from its power. True repentance thus actually makes it impossible for a believer in Christ to continue living in sin. The love of Christ supplies the grand motivation for a change in the life (2 Corinthians 5:15). One finds a kind of joy in the experience:

> The sadness that is used by God brings a change of heart that leads to salvation—and there is no regret in that! But sadness that is merely human causes death. See what God did with this sadness of yours: how earnest it has made you. … Such indignation, such alarm, such feelings, such devotion. (2 Corinthians 7:10, 11, TEV).

Peter is another example of genuine repentance. We can identify with him, for he failed miserably, yet he found the precious gift of repentance which Judas refused. After basely denying his Lord with cursing, Peter "went out, and wept bitterly" (Mark 14:71; Luke 22:62). His repentance never ceased, for there was always afterward a tear glistening in his eyes as he thought of his sin in comparison with the Lord's kindness to him. But they were happy tears. The tempest of contrition always brings a rainbow glorified with the sunshine of divine forgiveness. Even medical scientists are beginning to recognize the wholesome healing therapy in tears of contrition, for men as well as for women. We ruin our health and shorten our lives when we resist or suppress the tenderness and melting influence of God's Spirit appealing to our hard hearts.

This Is Solid Happiness

Far from being a negative experience, such repentance is the foundation of all true joy. As every credit must have a corresponding debit to balance the books, so the smiles and happiness of life, in order to be meaningful, must be founded on the tears of Another upon whom was laid "the chastisement of our peace" and with whose "stripes we are healed" (Isaiah 53:5).

Repentance is not our tears and sorrow balancing the books of life; it is our appreciation of what it cost Him to bear our griefs and carry our sorrows (verse 4).

> The nearer we come to Jesus, and the more clearly we discern the purity of His character, the more clearly shall we see the exceeding

sinfulness of sin, and the less shall we feel like exalting ourselves. There will be a continual reaching out of the soul after God, a continual, earnest, heartbreaking confession of sin and humbling of the heart before Him (*Acts of the Apostles*, p. 561).

At every advance step in Christian experience our repentance will deepen. It is to those whom the Lord has forgiven, to those whom he acknowledges as His people, that He says, "Then shall ye remember your own evil ways, and your doings that were not good, and shall loathe yourselves in your own sight" (Ezekiel 36:31). (*Christ's Object Lessons*, pp. 160, 161).

A repentance like this is beyond us to invent or to initiate. It must come as a gift from above. God has exalted Christ "to give repentance to Israel" (Acts 5:31). And to the Gentiles also He "granted repentance unto life" (chapter 11:18). Is He any less generous to us today? The capacity for such a change of mind and heart is a priceless treasure worth more than all the millions in Las Vegas. Even the will to repent is His gift, for without it we are "dead in trespasses and sins" (Ephesians 2:1).

Such an experience seems almost wholly out of place in these last decades of the 20th century. Can a sophisticated church ever receive it?

What Makes Repentance Possible?

The Bible links together "repentance toward God and faith toward our Lord Jesus Christ" (Acts 20:21). Repentance is not a cold calculation of options and their consequences. It is not a selfish choice to seek an eternal reward or to flee the pains of hell. It is a heart experience that results from appreciating the sacrifice of Christ. It cannot be imposed by fear or terror, or even by hope of immortality. Only "the goodness of God leadeth thee to repentance."

The ultimate source from which this superb gift flows is the truth of Christ's sacrifice on the cross. As faith is a heart-appreciation of the love of God revealed there, so repentance becomes the appropriate exercise of that faith which the believing soul experiences. We follow where faith leads the way as illuminated by the cross—down on our knees. Peter's call to "repent, and be baptized every one of you" followed the most convicting sermon on the cross that has ever been preached (Acts 2:16-38). The phenomenal response at Pentecost was the fulfillment of Jesus' promise: "I, if I be lifted up from the earth, will draw all … unto Me" (John 12:32).

Why don't we see more of this precious gift? Is modern man too sophisticated to welcome it? No, human nature is not beyond redemption, even in these last days. Genuine repentance with "works meet for repentance" is rare only because that genuine preaching of the cross is rare (cf. Acts 26:20; 2 Corinthians 5:14). It is not out of date. Its essence is powerfully set forth in Isaac Watts memorable words:

> When I survey the wondrous cross
>   On which the Prince of glory died,
> My richest gain I count but loss
>   And pour contempt on all my pride.

Millions of people have personally repented since Pentecost. All through past ages, believing sinners have individually received the gift. Sleeping in the dust of the earth, they all await the "first resurrection." Theirs has been one phase of repentance.

However, there must be a second coming of Christ, or this all-important resurrection can never take place. Until then, all these dead saints are hopeless prisoners. Furthermore, without a preparation for His coming on the part of His living people, He cannot come. Therefore, until He comes, those sleeping saints of all ages who personally repented are doomed to remain in their dusty graves. This means that there must be a special repentance on the part of the "remnant," a key to unlock this log-jam of last day events. It is the heart-preparation of a people for translation without seeing death. This is unique in all history, and it is the reason for the existence of the Seventh-day Adventist Church. Otherwise, we have been sadly deceived for over a century.

What Is Different About Laodicea's Repentance?

Laodicea is not innately worse than the other six churches. But she is living in the last days, the time of the cleansing of the heavenly sanctuary. This never-before phase of our great High Priest's Day of

Atonement ministry calls for a never-before kind of response from us. This becomes another phase of repentance.

Laodicea is far behind the times in which she lives. In Christ's view, her spiritual condition has become an anachronism. She is "wretched, and miserable, and poor" in a time when she should enjoy unprecedented spiritual wealth. If we, accustomed to today's technology, were suddenly to return to living like a king in the Dark Ages, we would be pitied as "wretched ... and poor," for we would have no plumbing, no electricity, no furnace, no car, no phone, no TV, no knowledgeable medical care. Hardly any reader of this book would willingly return to such a primitive life, even in a medieval palace, with chamber-pots, spit-baths, and exposure to the Great Plague.

Jesus says that Laodicea is "wretched" because the spiritual wealth of past ages becomes "miserable" poverty in a time when true spiritual wealth is possible beyond any previous age. While Christ is performing His "final atonement" in the second apartment of the heavenly sanctuary, can we continue living as though He were still in the first apartment? The gap between Laodicea's unique opportunities and her true state has widened so much that her pathetic condition has become the most difficult problem the Lord has ever had to deal with.

If her condition is unique, surely the repentance Christ calls for from her must also be unique. The repentance Laodicea needs will fit the glorious potential of the heavenly Day of Atonement, because the message to Laodicea parallels this cleansing of the sanctuary. We must discover what this means in practical, understandable terms.

Repentance and the Cleansing of the Sanctuary

The blotting out of sins takes place in "the times of refreshing," that is, the cleansing of the sanctuary (see Acts 3:19). The "daily" ministry included the forgiveness of sins, but the "yearly" goes further.

This Day of Atonement ministry of blotting out sins can occur only at the end of time, after the conclusion of the 2300 years (see *The Great Controversy*, pages 421, 422, 483). In these last days there is something Laodicea "knows not," some deeper level of guilt which has never been discerned. Here is where that deeper repentance is needed.

It will not suffice for us to say, "Let the heavenly computers do the work—our sins will be blotted out when the time comes without our knowing about it." There is no such thing as automatic, computerized blotting out of sins that takes place without our participation and cooperation. It is we who are to repent individually and understandably, not the heavenly computers.

A little thought will make it clear that no sin can be "blotted out" unless we come to see it and confess it understandably. Our deeper level of sin and guilt must be realized if our Saviour's complete ministry for us is to be appreciated. Nothing short of this can be adequate repentance in such a time as this. This experience is related to the Day of Atonement.

Hence there lies before Laodicea an experience of repentance that is unique in world history. All things are being held up for lack of it. Our plane is freighted with the precious cargo of the Loud Cry "good news" message to enlighten the earth. But it has been going in circles in a holding pattern. There is no time now for more delay, not even to wait for persecution, for then it may be too late.

The principle of a deeper layer of guilt beneath the surface is made clear in many inspired statements. Here are a few:

> The work of restoration can never be thorough unless the roofs of evil are reached. Again and again the shoots have been clipped, while the root of bitterness has been left to spring up and defile many; but the very depth of the hidden evil must be reached, the moral senses must be judged, and judged again, in the light of the divine presence (*Bible Commentary*, Vol. 5, p. 1152).

> The Laodicean message must be proclaimed with power; for now it is especially applicable. ... Not to see our own deformity is not to see the beauty of Christ's character. When we are fully awake to our own sinfulness, we shall appreciate Christ. ... Not to see the marked contrast between Christ and ourselves is not to know ourselves. He who does not abhor himself cannot understand the meaning of redemption. ... There are many who do not see themselves in the light of the law of God. They do not loathe selfishness; therefore they are selfish (*Review and Herald*, September 25, 1900).

The message to the Laodicean church reveals our condition as a people. ... Ministers and church-members are in danger of allowing self to take the throne. ... If they would see their defective, distorted characters as they are accurately reflected in the mirror of God's word, they would be so alarmed that they would fall upon their faces before God in contrition of soul, and tear away the rags of their self-righteousness (*Ibid.*, December 15, 1904).

The Holy Spirit will reveal faults and defects of character that ought to have been discerned and corrected. ... The time is near when the inner life will be fully revealed. All will behold, as if reflected in a mirror, the working of the hidden springs of motive. The Lord would have you now examine your own life, and see how stands your record with Him (*Ibid.*, November 10, 1896).

If we have defects of character of which we are not aware, He [the Lord] gives us discipline that will bring those defects to our knowledge, that we may overcome them. ... Your circumstances have served to bring new defects in your character to your notice; but nothing is revealed but that which was in you (*Ibid.*, August 6, 1889; all emphasis in above quotations is supplied). There is nothing "negative" in these quoted paragraphs. If one were sick with a fatal cancer, one would welcome as precious good news the surgeon's announcement that surgery to remove the cancerous tissue is possible.

The Greatest Sin of All the Ages

What brought ancient Israel's ruin? She refused to accept her Messiah's message which exposed a deeper level of guilt than she had previously realized. The Jews of Christ's day were not by nature more evil than any other generation; it was simply theirs to act out to the full the same enmity against God that all the fallen sons and daughters of Adam have always had by nature. The divine Son of God came to them on a mission of mercy. As our natural "carnal mind is enmity against God" (Romans 8:7), they simply demonstrated this fact visibly in the murder of their divine Visitor. Those who crucified the Saviour hold up a mirror wherein we can see ourselves.

Horatius Bonar learned this in a dream in which he seemed to be witnessing the crucifixion. In a frenzy of agony, as in a nightmare, he tried to remonstrate with the cruel soldiers who were driving spikes through Christ's hands and feet. He laid his hand on the shoulder of one to beg him to stop. When the murderer turned to look at him, Bonar recognized his own face.

Laodicea's repentance will go down to the deepest roots of this natural "enmity against God." This deeper phase of repentance is repenting of sins that we may not have personally committed, but which we would have committed if we had the opportunity. The root of all sin, its common denominator, is the crucifixion of Christ. A repentance for this sin is appropriate because the books of heaven already record this sin written against our names:

> That prayer of Christ for His enemies embraced the world. It took in every sinner that had lived or should live. … Upon all rests the guilt of crucifying the Son of God (*The Desire of Ages*, p. 745).
>
> God's law reaches the feelings and motives, as well as the outward acts. It reveals the secrets of the heart, flashing light upon things before buried in darkness. God knows every thought, every purpose, every plan, every motive. The books of heaven record the sins that would have been committed had there been opportunity (*Bible Commentary*, Vol. 5, p. 1085).

"Opportunity" has come to others in the form of alluring, overmastering temptations through circumstances we ourselves may not have encountered. None of us can endure the full consciousness of what we would do if under sufficient pressure—terrorism, for example. (The enforcement of the "mark of the beast" will surely provide the ultimate "opportunity.") But our potential sin is already recorded in "the books of heaven."

A Jewish concentration camp survivor of the Holocaust discovered this truth in an unusual way. Yehiel Dinur walked into the Nuremburg court in 1961, prepared to testify against Nazi butcher Adolf Eichmann. But when he saw Eichmann in his humbled status, Dinur suddenly began to cry, then fell to the floor. It was not hatred or fear which overcame him. He suddenly realized that Eichmann was not the superman that the inmates had feared; he was an ordinary man. Says Dinur: "I was afraid about myself. I saw that I am capable to do this. I am ... exactly like he!" Mike Wallace of "60 Minutes" told the story on TV. He summed it up: "Eichmann is in all of us."

Only the full work of the Holy Spirit can bring to us the full conviction of the reality of sin; but in these last days when sins must be "blotted out" as well as pardoned, this is His blessed work. No buried bacteria or virus of sin can be translated into God's eternal kingdom.

The Laodicean call to repentance is the essence of the message of Christ's righteousness. Whatever sins other people are guilty of, they obviously had the "opportunity" of committing them; somehow the temptations were overmastering to them. The deeper insight the Holy Spirit brings to us is that we are by nature no better than others. Christ's righteousness is 100% imputed to us; we don't have even one percent that is ours by nature. When Scripture says that "all have sinned," it means, as the New English Bible translates it, "all alike have sinned" (Romans 3:23). Digging down to get the roots out—this is now "present truth."

There is no way that we can appreciate the heights of Christ's glorious righteousness until we are willing to recognize the depths of our own sinfulness. For this reason, to see our own potential for sin is inexpressibly good news!

> I take, O cross, thy shadow for my abiding place;
>   I ask no other sunshine than the sunshine of His face,
> Content to let the world go by, to know no gain nor loss,
>   My sinful self my only shame, my glory all the cross.
>   (Elizabeth Clephane)

A confession of sin that only scratches the surface can produce only a surface or veneer forgiveness. And that, of course, produces spiritual lukewarmness.

What are the practical aspects of this ultimate disclosure of our true guilt, and of God's more abounding grace that cleanses it?

Our search must continue.

Chapter 4

How A Deeper Repentance
Pervades The "Body"

The 17th century poet John Donne grasped the truth I am trying to express:

> No man is an island, entire of itself; every man is a piece of the continent, a part of the main; if a clod be washed away by the sea, Europe is the less, as well as if a promontory were, as well as if a manor of thy friends or of thine own were; any man's death diminishes me, because I am involved in mankind; and therefore never send to know for whom the bell tolls; it tolls for thee (Devotions, XVII).

It would have been only a short step more for Donne to have said, "Any man's sin diminishes me, because I am involved in mankind; and therefore never send to know who crucified the Christ; it was thou."

A person is more than a scattered assortment of limbs, organs, and cells. These parts of a "body" thrive on a vital relationship together. None could survive alone. Such is the church. Christ is "the Head," and we are all individually "members of His body."

No individual believer in Christ can reveal all the infinite facets of His character. Neither can a single part of one's physical body fulfill all of the intents of the head. The feet can do things the hands can't do, and vice versa. Each of us in the church is needed.

The apostle Paul grasped the idea of this vital member-to-member- to-Christ relationship. Truly inspired by the Holy Spirit, his simple illustration is brilliant. It is almost as if the human body had been created just to provide this perfect symbol of the relationship the church bears to the world and to Christ:

Christ is like a single body with its many limbs and organs, which, many as they are, together make up one body. ... A body is not a single organ, but many. ... God appointed each limb and organ to its own place in the body, as He chose. If the whole were one single organ, there would not be a body at all; in fact, however, there are many different organs, but one body. ... God has combined the various parts of the body, giving special honour to the humbler parts, so that there might be no sense of division in the body, but that all its organs might feel the same concern for one another. If one organ suffers, they all suffer together. ... Now you are Christ's body, and each of you is a limb or organ of it (1 Corinthians 12:12-27, NEB).

The Meaning of the Word "Corporate"

The word "body" is a noun, and the word "bodily" is an adverb; but there is no meaningful English adjective that can describe the nature of this relationship within the "body" except the word "corporate" from the Latin word for body, *corpus*.

The dictionary defines it as "relating to a whole composed of individuals." Your own experience can make this plain.

What happens when you stub your toe badly? At once you realize the corporate relationship of the limbs and organs of your body. You stop while your whole body cooperates in an effort to rub the hurting toe and lessen the pain. You may even hurt all through your body. Your other organs and limbs feel a corporate concern for that wounded toe, as if each feels the pain.

The other members may be thought of as feeling responsible for the wound, the leg saying, "Had I been more careful, the toe would not have been stubbed," or the eye saying, "If I had been more watchful, it wouldn't have happened." "If one organ suffers, they all suffer together" (1 Corinthians 12:26, NEB.) The idea of corporate responsibility is implicit in Paul's inspired illustration.

Any illness or amputation in the body becomes a "schism" to be avoided at almost any cost. Likewise, any measure of disunity or misunderstanding, or lack of compassion in the church, is foreign to

Christ and His body. It is as alien as disease or accident is to our human body. Sin is such an accident to the "body of Christ," and guilt is its disease.

Often we suffer disease without knowing which organ is ill, or even what causes it. Could our Laodicean disease of luke-warmness be something similar? What is the spiritual virus that perpetuates it? How can it have both a personal and corporate nature?

Are Some Lions "Good" and Some "Bad"?

A few lions in Africa become man-eaters, but the vast majority never get a taste of human beings. Does this mean that most lions are "good" and only a few are "bad"?

There is no difference so far as lion "character" is concerned. All lions are alike, and given the proper circumstances, any lion will be a man-eater. When it becomes weak or old, separated from the pride which would normally supply it with food, it readily turns to man-eating. We noticed in our last chapter Ellen White's disturbing statement, "The books of heaven record the sins that would have been committed had there been opportunity." A man-eating lion is simply acting out its basic nature and we can be thankful that most of them don't get the "opportunity" to demonstrate it fully!

What is our basic nature as sinners? The answer is unpalatable to recognize. We are at enmity with God by nature, and await only the proper circumstances to demonstrate it. Crucifying the Son of God is its ultimate measure.

A familiar disease may illustrate how sin operates in human nature. In malarial areas, people are bitten by the anopheles mosquito, and infected with the disease. Some ten days after the bite, the parasites in the blood stream produce malarial fever. Not only is the one "member" such as the finger affected which received the mosquito bite, but the whole body partakes of the common fever. The blood stream has carried the parasites everywhere. *This is a corporate disease.*

When we receive an injection of an anti-malarial drug in one "member," the arm receiving it is not the only member to benefit. The medicine begins to course throughout the blood stream. Soon the entire body is healed of the disease, and the fever disappears over all the body, not just in the one "member." *This is a corporate healing.*

In order to understand what full repentance is, we need to understand our relationship to the entire human race "in Adam." The Bible considers the whole human race to be one man—Adam. But Christ came to take Adam's place; when He died on the cross, the whole world died with Him, in principle. As one's entire body feels the fever of the malarial infection, so did Christ feel the weight of the sins of the world. This we must appreciate, if we are to appreciate His healing. As long as we feel that we have escaped the infection of the common parasite of sin "in Adam," we shall feel superior to others simply because the infection happened not to occur in our particular "member." Then we fail to share in the full corporate healing provided by Christ.

We are powerless to help someone find deliverance from his sin if in superiority we fail to sense the weight of his guilt. In order to feel this weight we do not need to repeat his sinful deed. By corporate repentance, we put ourselves in his place. This is not difficult; as we shall see, Christ has shown us the way. What is needed is to see and appreciate Christ more fully!

A Portrait of Christ and of His Body

Marvelous will be the results when God's people as a church learn to feel for the world as Christ feels for it. The only way He has to show His love is through us. This is why "God hath set ... in the church" the various gifts of His Spirit so that the church may become His efficient "body" for expressing Himself to the world, as a healthy person expresses through his physical members the thoughts and intent of his mind. These "gifts" lead up to the supreme gift of love, which Paul says is "a more excellent way."

First Corinthians 12 discusses the corporate relationship of the "many members" with one another and with Christ. This leads to the supernatural love revealed in chapter 13. Such love is not to be thought impossible to achieve. It is the normal function of the "body," its corporate effectiveness in service.

Many have seen in chapter 13 a "portrait" of Christ. But in its full context the love portrait really is that of the church. Paul combined the 13th with the 12th chapter in order to demonstrate how the union of the "many members" with Christ works out in practical life. It is possible for this to be fully realized now.

When the "many members" express His love to our dark world, the lines will be clearly drawn. Everyone will decide for or against this final revelation of love. The score can be announced, for the game will then be over. Thus the Lord's prophecy will be fulfilled through personal witness: "This gospel of the kingdom shall be preached in all the world for a witness to all nations; and then shall the end come" (Matthew 24:14).

The physical body is created so that each member cooperates in perfect unity. "So also is Christ. ... There should be no schism [paralysis] in the body; ... the members should have the same care one for another" (1 Corinthians 12:12, 25). No breakdown of vital nerve pathways severs this unity. The Day-of-Atonement-repentance is the nerve pathway that will communicate an effective love to every member of Christ's body who is willing to receive the gift.

Chapter 5

Christ's Repentance For Sins
He Never Committed

Both the Bible and Ellen White's writings make it clear that Jesus Christ experienced repentance. But it seems almost preposterous to imagine how or why Jesus could experience repentance!

This does not mean that He experienced sin, for never in thought, word, or deed did He yield to temptation. Peter says of Him, "Who did no sin, neither was guile found in His mouth" (1 Peter 2:22).

If John the Baptist "baptized with the baptism of repentance" (Acts 19:4), he must have baptized Jesus with the only baptism he knew—one that implied on the part of the sinless Candidate an experience of repentance. Otherwise, the baptism would have been a farce, and both John and Jesus would be guilty of hypocrisy. That is unthinkable.

But how could Christ experience repentance if He had never sinned? We have assumed that only evil people need to repent, or can repent. It is shocking to think that good people can repent, and incomprehensible how a perfect Person could repent.

Nevertheless, if Christ was "baptized with the baptism of repentance," it is clear that He did experience repentance. But the only kind a sinless person could experience is corporate repentance. Thus, Jesus' repentance is a model and example of the kind He expects of Laodicea. It has special meaning for us who live in the end-time Day of Atonement.

Christ's Repentance For Sins He Never Committed

Jesus was sincere when He asked John to baptize Him. John was also sincere in refusing. The prophet obviously did not understand the principle of corporate guilt and repentance. But Jesus explained the reason for His request for baptism. He answered the prophet's objections at the Jordan, "Thus it becometh us to fulfill all righteousness" (Matthew 3:15).

It's impossible to imagine that He was suggesting that He and John should together merely act out a play. The essence of "righteousness" is sincerity and genuineness. Our divine Example could never condone a performance without the appropriate experience of heart. Play-acting could never "fulfill all righteousness." For Christ to subject Himself to baptism without an experience appropriate to the deed would have been to give an example of hypocrisy, the last thing Jesus wants from anyone! Never does He want anyone to experience the act of baptism without true repentance.

Was Jesus' baptism a legalistic provision, a deposit of merit to be drawn on in a substitutionary way in emergencies? Occasionally people such as the thief on the cross can not for physical reasons be baptized. One must be baptized in order to enter Paradise. The poor thief nailed to a cross cannot be immersed; Jesus' baptism thus helps him out like a credit transfer in a bank transaction, and the appropriate "deposit" is placed to the account of the unbaptized thief. Is this "bank" of merit the purpose of Christ's baptism? Many have thought so, but this can not be true. Such legalistic shenanigans are foreign to the spirit of the gospel.

If any valid element lurks in this puerile concept, the idea leaves us cold. Most people have had opportunity to be immersed, and believers have complied. What then could Jesus' baptism mean to them? Is it merely a physical demonstration by the Teacher showing the right method?

Once the truth of corporate repentance is recognized, Jesus' baptism begins to make sense.

How Close Jesus Came to Us

Jesus asked for baptism because He genuinely identified Himself with sinners. If Adam represents the entire human race, Jesus became the "last Adam," taking upon Himself the guilt of humanity's sin. Not that He sinned, but He felt how the guilty sinner feels. He put Himself fully in our place. He put His arms around us as He knelt down beside us on the banks of the Jordan, asking His Father to let Him be the Lamb of God. His submission to baptism indicates that "the Lord ... laid on Him the iniquity of us all." His baptism therefore becomes an injection of healing repentance for sin into the body of humanity. Peter says that His identity with our sins was deep, not superficial, for "His own self bare our sins in His own body" (Isaiah 53:6; 1 Peter 2:24).

Christ did not bear our sins as a man carries a bag on his back. In His own "flesh," in His soul, in His nervous system, in His conscience, He bore the crushing weight of our guilt. So close did He come to us that He felt as if our sins were His own. His agony in Gethsemane and on Calvary was real.

Ellen White offers these perceptive comments on Christ experiencing this deep heart-repentance in our behalf:

> After Christ had taken the necessary steps in repentance, conversion, and faith in behalf of the human race, He went to John to be baptized of him in Jordan (*General Conference Bulletin*, 1901, p. 36.)

> John had heard of the sinless character and spotless purity of Christ. ... John could not understand why the only sinless one upon the earth should ask for an ordinance implying guilt, virtually confessing, by the symbol of baptism, pollution to be washed away. ...

> Christ came not confessing His own sins; but guilt was imputed to him as the sinner's substitute. He came not to repent on His own account; but in behalf of the sinner. ... As their substitute, He takes upon Him their sins, numbering Himself with the transgressors, taking the steps the sinner is required to take; and doing the work the sinner must do (*Review and Herald*, January 21, 1873.)

This may be perplexing. Let us take a second look:

(a) Though Christ was utterly sinless, He did in His own soul experience repentance. The statements are repeated, and there is a Biblical basis for them.

(b) His baptism shows that He knows exactly how "every repenting sinner" feels. In our self-righteousness we cannot feel such sympathy with "every repenting sinner." That's one big reason why we win so few souls. Only a Perfect Person can experience a perfect and complete repentance such as that.

(c) His taking "the steps the sinner is required to take" underscores His identity with us. We cannot in truth "behold the Lamb of God which taketh away the sin of the world" without grasping how close He has come to us. This is why it is so necessary to "behold" Jesus. Lukewarm impenitence is due either to not seeing Him clearly revealed, or to rejecting Him. To take a closer look at "the Lamb of God" is to understand what is our deep sin that needs to be "taken away."

Why did Jesus in His ministry have such phenomenal power to win human hearts? In His pre-baptism "repentance, conversion, and faith in behalf of the human race," He learned to know what was "in man," for "he needed not that any should testify of man" (John 2:25). This is how He learned to speak as "never man spake" (John 7:46). Only thus could He break the spell of the world's enchantment so He could say to whom He would, "Follow Me," passing by no human being as worthless, inspiring with hope the "roughest and most unpromising.'" To such a one, discouraged, sick, tempted, fallen, Jesus would speak words of tenderest pity, words that were needed and could be understood" (*Ministry of Healing*, p. 26). We can begin to see that we ourselves can never know such drawing power with people until we have experienced the kind of repentance that Christ experienced in our behalf.

The "How" of Jesus' Power to Reach Hearts

Jesus' perfect compassion for every human soul is a direct result of His perfect repentance in behalf of every human soul. He becomes the second Adam, partaking of the body, becoming one with us, accepting us without shame, "in all things ... made like unto His brethren" (Hebrews 2:17).

We freely recognize our need of this genuine, unfailing Christ-like love in order to be a caring church. But we can preach about it for a thousand years and never get it, except through the mature faith that comes with Laodicea's final repentance. And such faith is a heartfelt appreciation of His true character, seen more clearly in its true dimensions. His repentance is a vital aspect of Immanuel's sinless character.

Through union with Him by faith we become part of the corporate body of humanity in Him. "As in Adam all die, even so in Christ shall all be made alive" (1 Corinthians 15:22). It is gross selfishness to want to appropriate Christ, yet refuse to appropriate His love for sinners.

In fact, we have infinitely more reason to feel close to them than did our sinless Lord, for we ourselves are sinners; but our human pride holds us back from the warm empathy that Christ felt. How to experience this closeness is the purpose of true repentance.

The first step must be to recognize our corporate involvement with the sin of the whole world. Although we were not physically present at the events of Calvary two thousand years ago, "in Adam" the whole human race was there. As surely as we are by nature "in Adam," so surely are we in Adam's sin.

How can this be? Suppose that we had no Savior. If any of us were left to develop to the full the evil latent in his own soul, if we were left to be tempted to the ultimate as others have been, we would surely duplicate the sin of others if given enough time and opportunity. That is, if there were no Saviour to save us from ourselves. Suppose Hitler had lived as long as Methuselah! No fallen member of the human race has any element of natural righteousness. There is no righteousness except that which is imputed and imparted by Christ. None of us dares to say, "I could never do what others have done!" And the sin of sins that underlies all sin, of which we are all alike guilty in a corporate sense, is the murder of the Son of God.

But how can we feel responsible for a sin committed by other people in another land two thousand years before we were born? The "good news" tells us that God forgives that sin, but how can we receive forgiveness for a sin we don't feel guilty of committing?

The apostle John tells us that it is only when we confess a sin that we can experience Christ's "faithful" forgiving and cleansing from it (1 John 1:9). But to confess a sin without sensing its reality becomes mere lip-service, perilously close to hypocrisy. Skin-deep confession and skin-deep repentance bring skin-deep love, skin-deep devotion.

Jesus teaches that we must realize we have been "forgiven much" before we can learn to "love much" (see Luke 7:47).

When Paul said, "I am crucified with Christ" (Galatians 2:20), he meant that he identified himself with Christ. In the same way we identify ourselves with Christ's repentance in behalf of the human race; the path to corporate repentance is in the footsteps of Christ.

The true dimensions of our sin begin to become apparent in the light of Christ's cross. Note how an inspired comment clearly discloses our ultimate sin, for which we can "individually repent":

> In the day of final judgment, every lost soul will understand the nature of his own rejection of truth. The cross will be presented, and its real bearing will be seen. ... Before the vision of Calvary with its mysterious Victim, sinners will stand condemned. ... Human apostasy will appear in its heinous character (*The Desire of Ages*, p. 58).

We are still in a world where Jesus, the Son of God, was rejected and crucified. ... Unless we individually repent toward ... our Lord Jesus Christ, whom the world has rejected, we shall lie under the full condemnation that the action of choosing Barabbas instead of Christ merited. The whole world stands charged today with the deliberate rejection and murder of the Son of God. ... Jews and Gentiles, kings, governors, ministers, priests, and people—all classes and sects who reveal the same spirit of envy, hatred, prejudice, and unbelief, manifested by those who put to death the Son of God—would act the same part, were the opportunity granted, as did the Jews and people of the time of Christ. They would be partakers of the same spirit that demanded the death of the Son of God (*Testimonies to Ministers*, p. 38).

These statements deserve a second look:

(a) Even "ministers" and church members partake of this guilt of crucifying Christ. Apart from the grace of God manifested through personal repentance, "every sinner" shares it.

(b) Without this grace, "every sinner" would repeat the sin of Christ's murderers if given enough time and opportunity.

(c) The sin of Calvary is an out-cropping of sinful alienation of which we are not aware, except by enlightenment of the Holy Spirit. At Calvary, every one's sin is fully unmasked.

(d) In a real sense we were each one at Calvary, not through pre-existence or pre-incarnation, but through corporate identity "in Adam." If it is true that "upon all rests the guilt of crucifying the Son of God," Adam likewise partakes of that guilt equally with us today. His sin in Eden was to Calvary what the acorn is to the oak.

(e) The "righteous" in their own eyes, including "ministers" and "priests" of "all ... sects," are potentially capable of revealing "the same spirit" as was manifested by those who actually crucified Christ. This must of course include our own denomination, except for the grace of repentance.

The little acorn of our "carnal mind" needs only enough time and opportunity to grow into the full oak of the sin of Calvary. This is the lesson of all history.

But he who has "the mind of Christ" will necessarily have also the repentance of Christ. Therefore, the closer he comes to Christ, the more he will identify with every sinner on earth through corporate repentance.

The apostle Paul was the first to articulate this brilliant idea of each individual believer relating to the body and the Head in a corporate sense. When his idea is recognized, we begin to feel that we too are "debtor both to the Greeks, and to the barbarians" (Romans 1:14). Since we become organically joined to Christ in faith, His concerns become ours, just like the concerns of one organ of the body become the concerns of all the other members of the body. Each believing member of the body longs to fulfill the intent of the Head, just as a violinist's fingers "long" to perform skillfully the intent of the violinist's mind. The miracle of miracles takes place in the heart and life of the one who believes the gospel: he begins to love like Christ loves and like Paul loved!

This experience cuts short a thousand painful battles with temptation. Through corporate union with Christ, we genuinely feel that nothing we possess is ours by right. All our struggles with materialism, love of the world, obsession with money and things, sensuality, self-indulgence, are transcended at last by the new compulsion of this liberating oneness of mind with Christ. Paul's "debtor" idea initiates this practical new love for others.

To make this very practical, we can ask: How did Christ love sinners? If He were to come into our churches today, we might be scandalized.

He "recognized no distinction of nationality, or rank or creed." He would "break down every wall of partition." In His example "there is no caste, [but] a religion by which Jew and Gentile, free and bond, are linked in a common brotherhood, equal before God. No question of policy influenced His movements. He made no difference between neighbors and strangers, friends and enemies. ... He passed by no human being as worthless, but sought to apply the healing remedy to every soul. ... Every neglect or insult shown by men to their fellow men, only made Him more conscious of their need of His divine-human sympathy. He sought to inspire with hope the roughest and most unpromising" (*Ministry of Healing*, pp. 25, 26).

This is the practical love that corporate repentance produces in human hearts that will receive the gift. No longer need we be helpless to reach others whose evil deeds we do not understand and pride ourselves on not having committed. The gap is bridged that insulates us from them.

Christ can exercise no healing ministry through those who are frozen in an unfeeling impenitence. He did no sin yet knew repentance. We too can feel a genuine compassion in behalf of others whose sins we may not personally have committed, whether for lack of opportunity or for lack of temptation of equal intensity. Forthwith our work for them comes alive, and our efforts become effective.

Of others in trouble we genuinely feel, "There but for the grace of God am I." They will immediately sense the reality of our identity with them in the same way that sinners sensed Christ's identity with them. They will begin to hear in our voices the echo of His voice.

Why Only a Perfect Person
Can Experience A Perfect Repentance

The more nearly Christlike a person is, the greater will be his experience of repentance. This is why only Christ is the perfect Example of corporate repentance. Never before in world history and never since has a human being offered to the Father such an offering of contrition for human sin. Because of His perfect innocence and sinlessness, only Christ could feel perfectly the weight of all human guilt.

Here is a beautiful expression of this truth:

> Man had separated himself at such a distance from God by transgression of His law, that he could not humiliate himself before God proportionate to his grievous sin. The Son of God could fully understand the aggravating sins of the transgressor, and in His sinless character He alone could make an acceptable atonement for man in suffering the agonizing sense of His Father's displeasure. The sorrow and anguish of the Son of God for the sins of the world were proportionate to His divine excellence and purity, as well as to the magnitude of the offense (*Selected Messages*, Book One, pp. 283, 284).

The 144,000 are said to be "without fault before the throne of God" (Revelation 14:5). Therefore they will be able at last to approach Christ's perfect example of repentance, although they are sinners by nature.

> At every advance step in Christian experience our repentance will deepen. It is to those whom the Lord has forgiven, to those whom he acknowledges as His people, that He says, "Then shall ye remember your own evil ways, and your doings that were not good, and shall loathe yourselves in your own sight." Ezekiel 36:31. (*Christ's Object Lessons*, pp. 160, 161).

Ellen White recognized the principle of corporate guilt and repentance. It has far-reaching implications:

> As we see souls out of Christ, we are to put ourselves in their place, and in their behalf feel repentance before God, resting not

until we bring them to repentance. If we do everything we can for them, and yet they do not repent, the sin lies at their own door; but we are still to feel sorrow of heart because of their condition, showing them how to repent, and trying to lead them step by step to Jesus Christ. (MS. 92, 1901; *Bible Commentary*, Vol. 7, p. 960).

However faint such a reflection may be, our repentance like this in behalf of others must be based on Christ's "repentance ... in behalf of the human race" (*General Conference Bulletin*, 1901, p. 36). It would be impossible for any of us to feel such concern and sorrow in behalf of others, had He not felt it first in our behalf.

If it is true that "we love because He first loved us," we can also say that we repent because He first repented in our "behalf." He is our Teacher.

Chapter 6

How Christ Called the Ancient Jews to National Repentance

Fresh from His own experience of corporate repentance and baptism "in behalf of the human race, " Jesus demanded the same from the Jewish nation: "From that time Jesus began to preach and to say, Repent: for the kingdom of heaven is at hand" (Matthew 4:17). And His disciples also "went out, and preached that men should repent" (Mark 6:12).

His greatest disappointment was the refusal of His nation to respond. He upbraided "the cities wherein most of His mighty works were done, because they repented not" (Matthew 11:20). The nation was likened to the unfruitful "fig tree planted in His vineyard ... Behold, these three years I come seeking fruit on this fig tree, and find none" (see Luke 13:6-9).

The barren fig tree which Jesus cursed (Mark 11:12-14) became a symbol representing not merely the mass of individual unrepentant Jews, but the corporate people which as a nation rejected Christ:

> The cursing of the fig tree was an acted parable. That barren tree, flaunting its pretentious foliage in the very face of Christ, was a symbol of the Jewish nation. The Savior desired to make plain to His disciples the cause and the certainty of Israel's doom (*Desire of Ages*, p. 582).

Our Lord has sent out the twelve and afterward the seventy, proclaiming that the kingdom of God was at hand, and calling upon men to repent and believe the gospel. ... This was the message borne to the Jewish nation after the crucifixion of Christ; but *the nation* that claimed to be God's peculiar people rejected the gospel brought to them in the power of the Holy Spirit (*Christ's Object Lessons*, p. 308; emphasis added.)

Note how personal sin had become national sin. It was accomplished by the nation's leaders and bound the nation to corporate ruin:

> When Christ came, presenting to the nation the claims of God, the priests and elders denied His right to interpose between them and the people. ... They set themselves to turn the people against Him (*Christ's Object Lessons*, pp. 304, 305).

How National Ruin Followed National Impenitence

Only national repentance could have saved the Jewish nation from the impending ruin which their national sin invoked upon them:

> For the rejection of Christ, with the results that followed, they were responsible. A *nation's* sin and a *nation's* ruin were due to the religious leaders (*Ibid.*, p. 305, emphasis added).
>
> Paul showed that Christ had come to offer salvation first of all to the *nation* that was looking for the Messiah's coming as the consummation and glory of their national existence. But that *nation* had rejected Him who would have given them life, and had chosen another leader, whose reign would end in death. He endeavored to bring home to His hearers the fact that repentance alone could save the Jewish nation from impending ruin (*Acts of the Apostles*, p. 247, emphasis added.)

Jesus' last public discourse was a final appeal to these leaders at the Jerusalem headquarters to repent. Their refusal called from Him a heartbroken lament. With tears in His voice, the Saviour predicted the national ruin impending: "All these things shall come upon this generation. O Jerusalem, Jerusalem ..." (Matthew 23:13-37).

There is a distinct difference between national repentance and personal repentance. Christ certainly appealed to individuals to repent. "Joy shall be in heaven over one sinner that repenteth" (Luke 15:7). He also appealed to "this wicked generation," that is, the nation. "The men of Nineveh shall rise up in the judgement with this generation, and shall condemn it: for they repented at the preaching of Jonas" (Luke 11:32). The fate of a nation, not merely that of individuals, was involved.

Like a lone flash of lightning on a dark night, this reference to Nineveh illustrates Jesus' idea. National repentance is so rare that few believe it can take place. Jesus used Nineveh's history as a ready example to show that what He was calling for was indeed possible. If a heathen nation can repent, He said in effect, surely the nation that claims to be God's chosen people can do the same!

> As Jonas was a sign unto the Ninevites, so shall also the Son of Man be to this generation. … The men of Nineveh shall rise up in the judgement with this generation, and shall condemn it: for they repented at the preaching of Jonas; and behold, a greater than Jonas is here (Luke 11:30, 32).

The "How" of Heathen Nineveh's Repentance

If one picture is worth a thousand words, Nineveh's repentance is a sharply focused illustration of a national response to the call of God. A nation repented, not simply a scattered group of individuals. It is easier for us to believe that the "great fish" swallowed Jonah alive than to grasp how a government and a nation actually repented at the preaching of God's word. "The people of Nineveh believed God, and proclaimed a fast, and put on sackcloth, from the greatest of them even to the least of them" (Jonah 3:5). There is no reason to doubt this sacred history.

This repentance began with "the greatest of them," and extended downward from the usual order in history to "the least of them." "Word came unto the King of Nineveh, and he arose from his throne, and he laid his robe from him, and covered him with sackcloth, and sat in ashes. And he caused it to be proclaimed and published through Nineveh by the decree of the king and his nobles." (Jonah 3:6, 7). It is true that this call to repent was not initiated at the royal palace.

But note that the government of Nineveh wholeheartedly supported it. The "city" repented from the top to the bottom. Fantastic! The repentance was both nationally "proclaimed and published," and individually received. The divine warning had proclaimed a corporate overthrow of Nineveh as a city; the people's repentance was complementary—a national repentance.

Jesus' point was this: if this happened once in history, why couldn't it happen with the Jews also?

Why couldn't the Jews have done as well as the heathen? Their national repentance would have been practical and easy to achieve. The high priest, Caiaphas could have led out as well as the king of Nineveh did. All Caiaphas needed was to accept the principle of the cross as Jesus taught it.

How Caiaphas Could Have Led Israel to Repentance

Even if he had sincerely not known how to relate to Jesus in the early days of the Saviour's ministry, he could at least at the time of Jesus' trial have taken a firm stand for right. A simple speech such as this to the Sanhedrin members was all he needed to make: "For a time I didn't understand the work of Jesus. You brethren have shared my misunderstanding. Something has been happening among us that has been beyond us. But I have studied the Scriptures lately. I have seen that beneath His lowly outward guise, Jesus of Nazareth is indeed the true Messiah. He fulfills the prophetic details. And now, brethren, I humbly acknowledge Him as such, and I forthwith step down from my high position and shall be the first to install Him as Israel's true High Priest."

A gasp of surprise would have rippled through the Sanhedrin chambers if Caiaphas had said these words, but he would today be honored all over the world as the noblest leader of God's people in all history. He would have done what Moses would have loved to do. The Jews, many of them, would doubtless have followed his lead. We have already seen how the religious leaders fastened on them a national guilt. It follows that these same leaders could also have led them into national repentance. Christ could have been offered in some other way than murder by His own people, and Jerusalem could today be the "joy of the whole earth" rather than its sorest plague spot.

If it should be that the remnant church today or in future should ultimately choose to follow ancient Israel in im-penitance, Christ would suffer at her hands the most appalling humiliation He has ever had to endure. He would be crucified afresh, wounded anew "in the house of His friends" (Zechariah 13:6). Humanity's final indignity would be heaped upon His sacrifice.

But there must be good news in God's word. The nature of Christ's sacrifice on the cross in relation to the antitypical Day of Atonement assures us that the church will at last overcome this tragic pattern. The church is His prized possession, which "he hath purchased with his own blood" (Acts 20:28). He is not to be ultimately cheated out of His reward.

For once in history, the history of God's people will not be repeated. Christ will be fully vindicated by them. An infinite price having been paid for their redemption, in the end it will be seen to be worthwhile. An infinite sacrifice will fully redeem and heal an infinite measure of human sin.

Though He was "a greater" than Jonah and "a greater than Solomon," Christ did not appear in the glorious garb and pomp of Solomon, nor did He "cause His voice to be heard in the streets" as did Jonah (cf. Matthew 12:42; Isaiah 42:2). But the Jewish leaders had evidence enough that Jesus was the true Messiah. This supreme evidence was inherent in the quality of His solemn call to repentance. No other "sign" was to be given that "evil and adulterous generation." Israel's frightful doom was just, because she refused to believe Heaven's last call to repentance. The surest evidence of the work of the true Holy Spirit today is to be seen in the quality of the True Witness' solemn call to us to repent.

The Ingathering of Repentant Jews

There remains a luminous hope for ancient Israel's literal descendants in our day:

> Blindness in part is happened to Israel, until the fulness of the Gentiles be come in. And so all Israel shall be saved. ... For the gifts and calling of God are without repentance. ... Through your mercy they also may obtain mercy (Romans 11:25-31).

It must be noted that a repentant Christian church is the key to the fulfillment of this prophecy! In the days before us we shall see some surprising developments among repentant Jews:

When this gospel shall be presented in its fulness to the Jews, many will accept Christ as the Messiah. ...

In the closing proclamation of the gospel, when special work is to be done for classes of people hitherto neglected, God expects His messengers to take particular interest in the Jewish people whom they find in all parts of the earth. ... This will be to many of the Jews as the dawn of a new creation, the resurrection of the soul. ... They will recognize Christ as the Saviour of the world. Many will by faith receive Christ as their Redeemer. ...

The God of Israel will bring this to pass in our day. His arm is not shortened that it cannot save. As His servants labor in faith for those who have long been neglected and despised, His salvation will be revealed (*Acts of the Apostles*, pp. 380,381).

How can we call Jews to such repentance unless we know the experience ourselves? God's great heart of pity is moved in behalf of these suffering people, and a great blessing is awaiting them when we are prepared to be the agents to bring it:

Notwithstanding the awful doom pronounced upon the Jews as a nation at the time of their rejection of Jesus of Nazareth, there have lived from age to age many noble, God-fearing Jewish men and women who have suffered in silence. God has comforted their hearts in affliction and has beheld with pity their terrible situation. He has heard the agonizing prayers of those who have sought Him with all the heart for a right understanding of His word (*Ibid.*, pp. 379, 380).

One's heart beats a little faster to read those words. They are pregnant with hope and wonder. What joy it will be to witness the fulfillment of our beloved Paul's bright visions of future restoration of the true Israel! Millions of Christians look to literal Israel in Palestine as the fulfillment. However, the servant of the Lord, in harmony with

Paul's concept of justification by faith, foresaw the genuine fulfillment in the Jews' repentance.

Could it happen in our time?

Yes, if we really want it. The Jews will be our pupils, to learn from us what they didn't learn two thousand years ago—how to repent.

Chapter 7

Ancient Israel's Full Cup of Impenitence

Could Jesus accuse people of a crime when they were innocent?

If someone accused me, for example, of starting World War I, I would respond that this was unreasonable. I wasn't even born when it started!

But Jesus accused the Jewish leaders of His day of guilt for a crime committed before any of them were born. His charge against them sounds unreasonable.

The story is in Matthew 23. Jesus has just upbraided the scribes and Pharisees with a series of "woes" accompanied by vivid flashes of irony and indignation. He concludes by springing on them this charge of murdering a certain Zacharias: "That upon you may come all the righteous blood shed upon the earth, from the blood of righteous Abel unto the blood of Zacharias son of Barachias, whom ye slew between the temple and the altar" (verse 35).

For years I assumed that this Zacharias was a victim whom Christ's hearers had personally murdered in the temple during their lifetime, not more than 30 or 40 years previous.

Human Guilt From A to Z

It was a shock to discover that this man was murdered some 800 years earlier. (The story is recorded in 2 Chronicles 24:20, 21). Why did Jesus charge the guilt of this crime on the Jews of His day?

When we see the principle of corporate guilt, the picture becomes clear. Jesus was not unfair. In rejecting Him, the Jewish leaders were acting out all human guilt from A to Z (Abel to Zacharias), even though they may not as yet have personally committed a single act of murder. They were in spirit one body with their fathers who had actually shed the blood of the innocent Zacharias in the temple. In other words, they would do it again, and they did do it—to Jesus.

Now, by refusing the call to repentance which the Baptist and Jesus had sent them, they had chosen to acquire the guilt of all murders of innocent victims ever since the days of Abel. One who could not err fastened the entire load on them.

Suppose the Jewish leaders had decided to repent? If so, they would have repented of "the blood of all the prophets, which was shed from the foundation of the world" (Luke 11:50). And thus they would not have gone on to crucify Christ. He could have been offered in some other way.

In order to understand how Jesus was thinking, we need to see clearly the Hebrew idea of corporate personality. The church is the "Isaac" of faith, Abraham's true descendant, "one body" with him and with all true believers of all ages. To Jewish and Gentile believers alike, Paul says Abraham is "our father" (Romans 4:1-13). To The Gentile believers he says, "Our fathers were ... all baptized unto Moses." "We [are] all baptized into one body, whether we be Jews or Gentiles" (1 Corinthians 10:1, 2; 12:13). We "all" means past generations and the present generation.

Christ's body is all who have ever believed in Him from Adam down to the last remnant who welcome Him at His return. All are one individual in the pattern of Paul's thinking.

Even a child can see this simple principle. Although it is his hand that steals from the cookie jar, when mother learns what happened, it's his bottom that gets the spanking. And to the child this is perfectly fair.

How a Man Paid Tithe Before He Was Born

So deeply imbedded in Paul's mind was this idea that he used a curious example to explain it. He said that Levi, Abraham's great-grandson, "paid tithes in Abraham." But when Abraham paid those tithes to Melchizedek, he as yet had no child at all. How could a distant seminal descendant of a yet childless ancestor possibly pay tithes? This sounds farfetched. Yet Paul dares to say that Levi paid tithes before even his own father Jacob had been begotten! "He was yet in the loins of his father [Abraham], when Melchizedek met him" (Hebrews 7:9, 10). Either Paul was ludicrously mistaken, or the Bible recognizes the principle of our corporate identity "in Abraham" and "in Christ."

The Old Testament develops this tremendous idea:

(a) **To Hosea, Israel through many generations is a single individual through youth and adulthood.** Israel "shall sing ... as in the days of her youth, and as in the days when she came up out of the land of Egypt" (Hosea 11:1; 2:15). Israel is personified as a girl who is to become a wife to the Lord.

(b) **To Ezekiel the history of Jerusalem is the biography of a single individual:**

> Thus saith the Lord God unto Jerusalem: thy birth and thy nativity is of the land of Canaan; thy father was an Amorite, and thy mother an Hittite. ... When I passed by thee, and looked upon thee, behold, thy time was the time of love. ... And thou wast exceedingly beautiful, and thou didst prosper into a kingdom. (Ezekiel 16:2-13).

Generations of Israelites may come and go, but her corporate personal identity remains. The guilt of "youth" is retained in adulthood, as an adult remains guilty of a wrong committed when he was a youth, even though physiologists say that every physical cell in his body had been replaced during intervening years. One's moral personal identity remains regardless of the molecular composition of the body.

(c) **Moses taught the same principle.** He addresses his generation as the "you" who should witness the fulfillment of his words in captivity to Babylon nearly a thousand years later (see Leviticus 26:3-40). He also called on succeeding generations to recognize their corporate guilt with "their fathers":

> If they shall confess their iniquity which they trespassed against me, and that they also have walked contrary to me; and that I also have walked contrary to them, and have brought them into the land

of their enemies; if then their uncircumcised hearts be humbled, and they then accept the punishment of their iniquity. ... I will for their sakes remember the covenant of their ancestors, whom I brought forth out of the land of Egypt (Leviticus 26:40-45).

(d) **Succeeding generations sometimes recognized this principle.** King Josiah confessed that "great is the wrath of the Lord that is kindled against *us*, because *our fathers* have not hearkened unto the words of this book, to do according unto all that which is written concerning us" (2 Kings 22:13). He said nothing about the guilt of his own generation, so clearly did he see their involvement with the guilt of previous ones.

(e) **Ezra lumps together the guilt of his generation with that of their fathers:** "Since the days of our fathers have we been in a great trespass unto this day; and for our iniquities have we, our kings, and our priests, been delivered into the hand of the kings of the lands" (Ezra 9:7, emphasis added). "Our kings" were those of previous generations, for there was no living king in Ezra's day.[1]

(f) **The David/Christ identity is striking.** David writes profound Psalms, expressing so perfectly what Christ was to experience that the Saviour used David's words to express the feelings of his own broken heart: "My God, My God, why hast Thou forsaken Me?" (Psalm 22:1; Matthew 27:46). Christ is the Word "made flesh." Nowhere is the perfect corporate identity of a "member" with the "Head" more clearly seen than in this David-Christ relationship. Christ knows Himself to be the "son of David." He has feasted on David's words and been inspired by David's experiences. The perfect identity He sees of Himself in the Old Testament in the experience and words of the prophets, becomes lived out in His own flesh through faith.

(g) **This idea of identity reaches a zenith in the Song of Solomon.** Here is the love story of the ages. Christ loves a "woman," even His church. Israel, the foolish "child" called out of Egypt, the fickle girl in her "time of love" in "youth," the faithless woman in the kingdom days, "grieved and forsaken" in the Captivity, at last becomes the chastened and mature "bride" of Christ. At last, through corporate repentance she is prepared to become a mate to Him.

Pentecost: Israel's History Not in Vain

Jesus was disappointed in His appeal to the Jews. Yet there did come at Pentecost a glorious demonstration of this principle of corporate repentance. His original appeal for national repentance was not entirely in vain.

It is hardly likely that the three thousand who were converted that day all personally shouted "Crucify Him!" at Christ's trial, or personally mocked Him as He hung on the cross. Peter's hearers recognized their shared guilt. Yet the Jewish leaders stubbornly refused to do so: "Did not we straitly command you that ye should not teach in this name? ... Ye ... intend to bring this man's blood upon us" (Acts 5:28). Their only hope would have been to recognize that His blood was on them!

Pentecost is a model inspiring God's people for nearly 2000 years. What made those grand results possible? The people believed the portrayal of their corporate guilt, and frankly confessed their part in the greatest sin of all ages.

The antithesis of Pentecost was the refusal of the Sanhedrin to accept Stephen's portrayal of corporate guilt through their national history: "Ye do always resist the Holy Ghost: as your fathers did, so do ye. Which of the prophets have not your fathers persecuted? and they have slain them which shewed before of the coming of the Just One; of whom ye have been now the betrayers and murderers" (Acts 7:51, 52). They "stopped their ears, and ran upon him with one accord, and cast him out of the city, and stoned him" (verses 57, 58).

Do we see the pattern that had been worked out? It began with Cain. Generation after generation refused to see their corporate guilt. Finally, impenitent Israel demonstrated to the world the tragic end that follows national impenitence. It's an unenviable distinction!

But in that tragic hour when Israel sealed her doom by murdering Stephen, a truth began to work itself out in an honest human heart that would lead to a correction of the sin of Israel. The "witnesses laid down their clothes at a young man's feet, whose name was Saul." This young man's disturbed conscience was to think through the great idea of a worldwide "body of Christ" which would eventually exhibit in full and final display the blessings of repentance which the Jews refused.

---

1. See Appendix C for a discussion of Ezekiel 18 and corporate guilt.

Chapter 8

Christ's Call To The Remnant Church To Repent

The "saints" who "keep the commandments of God and the faith of Jesus" (Revelation 14:12) are not independent, nondenominated, unorganized individuals. They are a body. Scattered limbs and organs are not a person. The denomination known as Seventh-day Adventists is recognized in the writings of Ellen White as the prophetic "remnant" church, and since our beginnings our pioneers have believed it to be the fulfillment of the Revelation prophecy. If this is not true, we have no authentic denominational identity, nor any true reason to exist:

In a special sense Seventh-day Adventists have been set in the world as watchmen and light-bearers. To them has been entrusted the last warning for a perishing world. ... They have been given a work of the most solemn import—the proclamation of the first, second, and third angels' messages. ...

The most solemn truths ever entrusted to mortals have been given to us to proclaim to the world. The proclamation of these truths is to be our work. The world is to be warned, and God's people are to be true to the trust committed to them (*Testimonies*, Vol. 9, p. 19. See *Testimonies*, Vol. 1, pp. 186, 187; *Selected Messages*, Book One, pp. 91-93; *Bible Commentary*, Vol. 7, pp. 959, 960, 961).

Insistent propaganda is assaulting the church from many sources, contending that the organized church has failed so badly that it has ceased to be the true prophetic remnant church. A misunderstanding of God's grace is the source of this separatist mentality. Critics and off-shoot enthusiasts do not understand the creative quality of God's agape love, nor the Bride-groom-bride symbolism of Scripture.[1] They do not see that the honor and vindication of Christ Himself are intimately involved in the repentance of the church. They see the sins of the church as unforgivable; they do not believe that denominational repentance is possible. Some sincere people who are ignorant of the message of Christ's righteousness become enticed by these siren messages and separate from the fellowship of the Seventh-day Adventist church.

This is unwise, it is unnecessary, and it is wrong. Christ never calls people to leave the church; He calls on us to repent. An inspired voice repeatedly and emphatically assures us of ultimate denominational repentance. This is implicit in statements like these:

I am instructed to say to Seventh-day Adventists the world over, God has called us as a people to be a peculiar treasure unto Himself. He has appointed that His church on earth shall stand perfectly united in the Spirit and counsel of the Lord of hosts to the end of time (Letter 54, 1908; *Selected Messages*, Book Two, p. 397).

Trust to God's guardianship. His church is to be taught. Enfeebled and defective though it is, it is the object of His supreme regard (Letter 279, 1904; *Ibid.*, p. 396).

While there have been fierce contentions in the effort to maintain our distinctive character, yet we have as Bible Christians ever been on gaining ground (Letter 170, 1907; pp. 396, 397).

The evidence we have had for the past fifty years [now 130] of the presence of the Spirit of God with us as a people, will stand the test of those who are now arraying themselves on the side of the enemy and bracing themselves against the message of God (Letter 356, 1907; p. 397).

The church may appear as about to fall, but it does not fall. It remains, while the sinners in Zion will be sifted out—the chaff separated from the precious wheat. This is a terrible ordeal, but nevertheless it must take place (*Ibid.*, p. 380).

Christ's Call To The Remnant Church

I am encouraged and blessed as I realize that the God of Israel is still guiding His people, and that He will continue to be with them, even to the end.

I am instructed to say to our ministering brethren, Let the messages that come from your lips be charged with the power of the Spirit of God. ... It is fully time that we gave to the world a demonstration of the power of God in our own lives and in our ministry (*Ibid.*, pp. 406, 407).

If the Seventh-day Adventist church has such a trust committed to her, it is equally true that Christ's message to Laodicea is addressed primarily to her. But notice that in Revelation 3:14-21, Christ is not speaking primarily to the church at large, but to its ministerial and administrative leadership:

(a) The Lord's greatest concern is for the leadership of His church. The book of Revelation is generally addressed "unto the seven churches," but the seven messages of chapters 2 and 3 are addressed particularly to the "angels of the seven churches."

(b) The word "angel" means messenger. It comes from *angello*, to deliver a message. The "angels of the seven churches" cannot be literal ones. These holy beings have neither left their "first love," nor "fallen," nor "suffered Jezebel to teach," nor lived a name when "dead," nor been "lukewarm." Neither do they need to "repent."

(c) These "angels" are precious to Jesus. He defines them as "the seven stars which thou sawest in My right hand" (Revelation 1:16, 20). Who are the "seven stars"? "God's ministers are symbolized by the seven stars. ... Christ's ministers are the spiritual guardians of the people entrusted to their care" (*Gospel Workers*, pp.13, 14). Theirs is serious business!

(d) We have seen that the Seventh-day Adventist Church is in a unique sense Laodicea. It follows that the "angel of the church of the Laodiceans" is primarily the responsible leadership of the Seventh-day Adventist church on all levels, each segment appropriately responsible. "These things, saith He that holdeth the seven stars in His right hand. These words are spoken to the teachers in the church—those entrusted by God with weighty responsibilities" (*Acts of the Apostles*, p. 586). They are "those whom God has appointed to bear the responsibilities of leadership" in the church, "those in the offices that God has appointed for the leadership of His people" (*Ibid.*, p. 164). If they refuse Christ's call, church organization must eventually disintegrate.

(e) The Laodicean message shows that Christ respects church organization. He intends that the "angel of the church" shall repent first, and then minister the experience to the worldwide church. The Laodicean message is evidence that this is His plan. (Suppose the leadership fails, or rejects the Lord's appeal? Israel's history demonstrates that "the people" can intervene and demand repentance; see Jeremiah 26).

If this were not true, He would have addressed the message "to the church of the Laodiceans," and disregarded "the angel of the church." Scripture and denominational history make this clear. When the leadership of the church "in a great measure" rejected the 1888 message (*Selected Messages*, Book One, pp. 234, 235), He did not disregard them; He permitted their failure to arrest the finishing of His work for a century. When Christ's appeal for repentance is appreciated, far more quickly than we think, contrition and reconciliation with Him will be communicated to the worldwide church. Hearts will be humbled before the Lord, and a people will be prepared for the close of probation. There is no reason why this vast task cannot be accomplished within our lifetime.

Will Christ Reject Laodicea?

The Laodicean message recognizes the church as Christ's one object of supreme regard. His appeal means that He has hope of success, that He fully expects His church to respond, else He would not waste his effort. His call expresses confidence in His church. Further, the time lapse of over a century indicates His patience and long-suffering which He could not bestow upon an object which He intended ultimately to abandon.

Thus the message to Laodicea is full of hope. Some are discouraged by the words, "Because thou art lukewarm ... I will spue thee out of my mouth" (Revelation 3:16). They feel that the church is so defective that Christ has already "spued" her out of His mouth, that is, rejected her; or that He will soon do so. They feel that the church is doomed, as surely and certainly as she is lukewarm. Didn't Christ promise His rejection of her?

The original language does not say unconditionally that Christ will reject His lukewarm church. What He said was, "I am about to spue thee out of my mouth" (*mello se emesai*). Since the apostle John wrote both the Revelation and the Gospel, we can better understand this expression by seeing how he used the same word *mello* ("I am about to") in another passage. Speaking of the "nobleman whose son was sick at Capernaum," John says that the son "was at the point of death" (John 4:47), using *mello*. What he says is that the boy was critically ill, about to die, but did not die.

What Jesus says to us is, "I am critically ill, suffering acute nausea on account of your lukewarmness," or, "You make Me sick." He does not say that the rejection is inevitable. Rather, He begs His church to heal His nausea by the only means practicable: "Be zealous, therefore, and repent."

The word "Laodicea" is not a dirty word, a synonym for failure. What's wrong with Laodicea is her lukewarmness, her blindness, her wretchedness, not her identity as the last of the seven churches. The name simply means "judging, or vindicating, the people."

Some individuals will never repent. Of them we read, "The figure of spueing out of His mouth means that He cannot offer up your prayers or your expressions of love to God. He cannot endorse your teaching of His word or your spiritual work in any wise. He cannot present your religious exercises with the request that grace be given you" (*Testimonies*, Vol. 6, p. 408). For some, perhaps for many, this rejection may have already taken place. What a pity for one to go on arrogantly as a leader, a pastor, a church officer, when Christ has nothing to do with him! But Christ's words do not predict a complete corporate failure of Laodicea.

Offshoots have occasionally arisen on the assumption that Christ has already rejected the entire leadership of His church. These grow out of a general misunderstanding of his call to repent. It is assumed that (a) the call to repent is for individual repentance; (b) it has been understood; and (c) it has been rejected. On the other hand, Scripture indicates that (a) the call is to corporate and denominational repentance; (b) history demonstrates that it has not been fully understood, and

(c) it has, therefore, not been rejected, at least not finally and intelligently.

If it should be eventually that Christ's call is rejected understandingly by His body, then the church would indeed be doomed. But that great "if" is not true. It would require the failure of the Laodicean message and the final defeat of the Lord Jesus as faithful Divine Lover. Everyone who is willing to concede such a defeat for Christ stands on the side of the enemy, for Satan is determined that such a defeat must take place. Even the nagging doubt that expresses the "if" is born of sinful, disloyal unbelief.

Satan constantly assailed the Son of God with barbed "ifs." "if He be the King of Israel," "if God will have Him," were torture to His soul. We are on Satan's side in the great struggle if we talk about "if the Bride repents and makes herself ready," or "if the church responds." That doubt of Christ's complete vindication paralyzes our devotion like nerve gas paralyzes a person's will. No one can work wholeheartedly for denominational repentance if he harbors the secret doubt that it is possible. This doubt underlies much of our present confusion, inertia, and disunity. But it is treason to Christ, as surely as were Judas' betrayal and Peter's denial of Him.

Is There a Remedy for Laodicea's Problems?

Christ's intent is that repentance be ministered throughout the church at large. Denominational pride and complacency are rebuked by the True Witness. Therefore, the remedy proposed is denominational repentance. The medicine must fit the disease.

We miss the point if we assume that His call is only for personal sin. It is true that we may individually battle for personal victory over evil temper, perverted appetite, love of amusement, pride of dress, sensuality, or thousands of other failings. But the point of the Lord's appeal in Revelation is that as a church and, more particularly as church leadership, we are guilty of denominational sin. This is specifically (a) denominational pride ("Thou sayest, I am rich and I have been enriched"); (b) denominational self-satisfaction ("Thou sayest, I have need of nothing"); (c) denominational self-deception ("Thou knowest not that thou art wretched"); and (d) denominational assumptions of success which are not divinely validated ("Thou art miserable, and poor, and blind, and naked").

The remedies proposed are: "gold tried in the fire," "white raiment," and "eyesalve." Upon the minds of church leadership there will be deeply impressed as never before in history a sense of our true role on the stage of the universe. The Lord's love for His last-day church finds expression not in pampering pride, but in His "faithful and true" rebuke and chastening, albeit with abundant evidence of loyalty.

We Must Succeed Where the Jews Failed

With the repentance of Nineveh standing in sacred history as the model, we see the pattern that the Lord expects to see develop today. "From the greatest of them to the least of them," the repentance in the Laodicean message must spread from the "top to the bottom" throughout the worldwide church. Unless Christ's sacrifice is in vain, it will come.

When this is understood and embraced by the "angel" of the church, the methods of its promotion will be uniquely effective. The Holy Spirit, not Madison Avenue promotional technique, will have "caused it to be proclaimed and published." As in Nineveh's day, "the king and his nobles" will range themselves solidly in support of what Christ calls for. (See Jonah 3:5-9). The principle makes every individual member to be vitally important, because corporate repentance does not criticize but works effectively by the faith of Christ. Although in the past the Lord's calls to repent have usually been refused, we must not expect that His final call will also fail. The prophetic picture is clear: something must happen in the end of time that has never happened before. The long sad history of millenniums of defeat must be reversed. This is required by the Bible doctrine of the cleansing of the sanctuary. The remnant church must glorify the Lord and vindicate Him in a way that has never yet been done. The key element will be a true and pure message of righteousness by faith.

Is the denominated Seventh-day Adventist Church the true "remnant" church? Or has its unfaithfulness and backsliding deprived it forever of the Lord's appointment as His true "remnant" church?

This question cannot be settled by the fallible method of considering the church's relative goodness or badness. Her identity does not depend on our subjective human judgment of her virtues or her failings. It depends on the objective criteria of Bible prophecy. Thus the real test of our faith is centered on Scripture itself. The prophecies of Daniel and Revelation pinpoint the rise of the last-day church commissioned to proclaim the everlasting gospel in its final setting. The history of the rise of this church demonstrates that it fulfills the criteria, however she may thus far have failed to accomplish her task.

The solution to the problem of her obvious infidelity is denominational repentance, not denominational disintegration. This is the experience that the High Priest ministers in the final Day of Atonement. Daniel's prophecy (8:14) declares that it "shall" take place, not perhaps or maybe. The time has come to believe the prophecy wholeheartedly, that we may unitedly cooperate with the High Priest in His task.

Thus the church will "make herself ready" to be the Bride of Christ. Doesn't He deserve this practical fruitage of His sacrifice? Hasn't He suffered enough, that at last His church shall give him the complete surrender that a bride gives to her husband? There are sincere church members who have doubted that such a repentance will ever take place. They need to understand that their doubting "ifs" are hindering the true work of God, and motivating souls to defect to the ranks of the one who is determined that Christ shall not be vindicated at last. The most serious problem the Lord has is not the outward enemies of His work, but the blindness and unbelief of His professed followers.

Can you think of any greater tragedy in the end of history than for a disappointed Christ to stand before "the door" knocking in vain and ultimately turning away in the humiliation of defeat? That's what the devil wants! Why should we give in to him by default? The picture we see in Revelation indicates complete success. "The sacrifices of God are a broken spirit: a broken and a contrite heart, O God, Thou wilt not despise" (Psalm 51:17). By virtue of the infinite sacrifice on Calvary, we must choose to believe that the Laodicean message will fully accomplish its objective.

Yes, the ancient Jews failed. But that does not mean that we today must fail. The impenitent "old Jerusalem" will become the penitent "New Jerusalem," both corporate bodies:

> That which God purposed to do for the world through Israel, the chosen nation, He will finally accomplish through His church on earth today. He has "let out His vineyard to other husbandmen," even to His covenant-keeping people, who faithfully "render Him the fruits in their seasons." (*Prophets and Kings*, pp. 713, 714).

Critics who have given up hope cannot see how God's love could possibly be loyal to such a faulty, erring church. They don't understand the true nature of love. They assume that divine love is like human love —conditioned by and dependent on the value or virtue of its object. (We fall in love with someone beautiful. We cannot comprehend falling in love with someone ugly). So critics look at the enfeebled and defective condition of the church and wonder how God's love for her can be permanent. "The church has failed," they say; "therefore, God's patient love must cease."

Divine love (*agape*), being free and independent, is not conditioned by the goodness or value of its object. It creates goodness and value in its object. It is this creative quality of divine love which guarantees the success of the message of the faithful and true witness to the angel of the church of the Laodiceans.

The Laodicean church is the new covenant church. Not for her own intrinsic goodness will the Lord remain loyal to her, but because He has to be a covenant-keeping God. "Not for thy righteousness, or for the uprightness of thine heart, dost thou go to possess their land: but ... [that] the Lord thy God ... may perform the word which the Lord sware unto thy fathers, Abraham, Isaac, and Jacob" (Deuteronomy 9:5).

We have no right to sit in judgment on our Lord's call, and deliberate over it as though it were a human suggestion someone makes. Perish the very thought! Is it not sufficient that the Lord calls for repentance? How dare anyone say, "Well, I like the idea, but doubt it will work," or, "In my opinion, we're not all that bad that we need denominational repentance." No committee or conference can dare to contradict Christ's call.

We read that "the Infinite One still keeps account with the nations. While His mercy is tendered with calls to repentance, this account remains open; but when the figures reach a certain amount which God has fixed, the ministry of His wrath begins. The account is closed." (*Prophets and Kings*, p. 364). If this is true, why can't He also keep an account with a denomination?

The universe of heaven is watching us on their equivalent of TV. They also watched the crucifixion of the Prince of glory. They have seen that He has called for a humbling of heart, contrition, melting of soul, from the denomination that prides itself on being "the remnant church."

What response will they see us make in our generation?

---

1. See Appendix B, page 103.

Chapter 9

How Can A Church Of Millions Of Members Repent?

How is it possible for a large organized church to repent? Does its complex machinery get in the way of the Holy Spirit's work? Must the body become spiritually more disjointed and uncoordinated, like a quadriplegic whose spasms and jerks are uncontrollable by the head? The Bible has an answer.

The essential quality of repentance remains the same in all ages and in all circumstances. People, not machines, not organizations, repent. But the repentance called for from Laodicea is unique in circumstances, depth, and extent. The church is not a machine, nor is its organization an impersonal force. The church is a body, and its organization is its vital functioning capacity. The individuals comprising this body can repent as a body.

As we have seen, metanoia (Greek for repentance) literally means perceptive "afterthought." It cannot be complete until the close of probationary history. Thus it cannot be complete until history's guilt is discerned. So long as a tomorrow may provide further reflection on the meaning of our "mind" today, or so long as another's sins may yet disclose to us our own deeper guilt, our repentance must remain to that extent incomplete.

But it will grow, for "at every advance step in Christian experience our repentance will deepen" (*Christ's Object Lessons*, p. 160). The High Priest who is cleansing the heavenly sanctuary has not abdicated His work. His people may fail to learn their lessons, but His patience will not fail. He will bring them back over the same ground to test them again and again until they overcome (*Testimonies*, Vol. 4, p. 214; Vol. 5, p. 623).

A Bright Future for God's Work

A beautiful experience is on the program of coming events, unique in history. Zechariah, Christ-centered prophet of last-day events, tells us that there will come to the last-day church and its leadership a heart-response to Calvary that will completely transform the church. Speaking of the final events, the prophet says:

And I will pour upon the house of David, and upon the inhabitants of Jerusalem, the spirit of grace and of supplications: and they shall look upon Me whom they have pierced, and they shall mourn for Him, as one mourneth for his only son. ... In that day there shall be a fountain opened to the house of David and to the inhabitants of Jerusalem for sin and for uncleanness (Zechariah 12:10-13:1).

Who are the "inhabitants of Jerusalem"? Jerusalem is a "city" of Abraham's descendants, the organized body of God's people. In Zechariah's day, Jerusalem meant a distinct group of people called to represent the true God to the nations of the world. Jerusalem was a corporate, denominated body of professed worshippers.

"The spirit of grace and supplications" is not to be poured out on scattered individual descendants of Abraham, but on the inhabitants of the "city," a visible body of God's denominated people on earth. It is implied that no descendant of Abraham choosing to dwell outside Jerusalem can share in it. Those Jews were indeed lost to history who chose to remain in the nations where they were scattered, refusing to move back to the ancestral nation in Palestine.

Who is "the house of David"? It was anciently the government of the denominated people of God. Zechariah refers to the leadership of the last-day church, or "the angel of the church," or "the king and his nobles," to borrow Jonah's terminology. They are "the men of Judah" whom Daniel distinguishes from "the inhabitants of Jerusalem" (Daniel 9:7). "The house of David" includes all levels of leadership in the organized church.

Does it seem impossible that a spirit of contrition shall be poured out on a leadership congested by organizational complexity? The more involved the church becomes with its multitudinous entities, the greater is the danger of its huge collective self choking the simple, direct promptings of the Holy Spirit. Each individual catching a vision is tempted to feel that his hands are tied—what can he do? The great organizational monolith, permeated with formalism and lukewarmness, seems to move only at a snail's pace. Aside from this "spirit of grace and supplications," the nearer we come to the end of time and the bigger the church becomes, the more complex and congested is its movement, and the more remote appears the prospect of repentance.

But let us not overlook what the Bible says. We need to remember that long before we developed our intricate systems of church organization, the Lord created infinitely more complex systems of organization, and yet "the spirit ... was in the wheels" (Ezekiel 1:20). Our problem is not the complexity of organization; it is the collective love of self. And the message of the cross can take care of that!

Why the Organization Is Needed

The world needs a "Jerusalem" as a "witness to all nations." Without her, the task cannot be done. The history of old Jerusalem's failure proves that without "the spirit of grace and of supplications," denominational organization inevitably becomes proud and misrepresentative of its divine mission. Zechariah says that a correct view of Calvary imparts contrition ("They shall look on Me whom they [not the Jews and Romans of a past millennium] have pierced"). The vision of the cross will provide the ultimate solution to the problem of human "sin and uncleanness."

What is "uncleanness"? It is that deeper layer of unrealized selfish motivation that underlies all sin, which must be cleansed in the Day of Atonement, but which has never been accomplished in any previous generation. The fear of hell, with the reverse side of the same coin, hope of eternal reward, will give way as motivation to the pure constraint of the love of Christ. The collective love of self will be "crucified with Christ."

What is "the spirit of grace and supplication"? Two distinct elements make up this phenomenal experience: "the spirit of grace," an appreciation of the cross, a view of God's character of love completely devastating and annihilating to human self-sufficiency and pride; and "the spirit of supplications," prayers arising from melted, contrite hearts. The difference in essential quality between these "supplications" and formal ordinary prayers is great. People will immediately detect the genuineness of these "supplications" because they will come from hearts humbled by corporate repentance. When prayer comes from such a heart, says David, then will we "teach transgressors Thy ways; and sinners shall be converted unto Thee" (Psalm 51:13).

The spirit pervading every congregation will be recognized. In close context to Zechariah's prophecy of chapter 10, we find another prophecy showing what will be the results of such denominational repentance:

People from around the world will come on pilgrimages and pour into Jerusalem from many foreign cities to attend these celebrations. People will write their friends in other cities [denominations] and say, "Let's go to Jerusalem to ask the Lord to bless us, and be merciful to us. I'm going! Please come with me. Let's go now!" (Zechariah 8:20, 21 Living Prophecies, paraphrased by Kenneth N. Taylor).

The Cross and Denominational Repentance

What can anyone do to hasten this day? Must we go into our graves and leave it to some future generation?

If we refuse the repentance Christ calls for, the answer must be, Yes. If we hold to "business-as-usual" pride and dignity, the answer must be, Yes. If we permit past negative patterns of denominational reaction to continue, the answer must be, Yes.

The answer to the question "How?" is the message of the cross. "They shall look on Me whom they have pierced," the Lord says. Here is focused the full recognition of corporate guilt; and the "spirit" bestowed can only follow a full, frank repentance of the body. All human sin centers in the murder of the Son of God. So long as this is not perceived, the "spirit of grace and supplication" is unwelcome to the proud heart and therefore not receivable. We then remain childish, tragically content to strut on the stage of the universe unaware of our true condition. A knowledge of the full truth brings sorrow for sin, not a self-centered fear of punishment, but a Christ-centered empathy for Him in His sufferings and a whole-hearted concern for His vindication.

This transfer of concern from self to Christ will be a miracle. It has never been fully realized since apostolic days. "They shall mourn for Him, as one mourneth for his only son, and shall be in bitterness for Him, as one that is in bitterness for his firstborn" (Zechariah 12:10). To shift our focus of concern from anxiety regarding our own salvation to such concern for Christ—this the Holy Spirit alone can accomplish. Our natural concern for our own personal security has often permeated our religious experience, our hymns, our prayers, our message. If there were no power of the Holy Spirit to accomplish the miracle of a change, we might estimate that decades, perhaps even centuries, would be needed to make such a change in human nature. But a "quick work" is possible, and has been promised.

The last church is composed of individuals like everyone else in human history, born with a "reprobate mind," the natural unregenerate heart of the sinner. But the revelation of truth will work for them a transformation of mind. The more fully the mind of Christ is received, the deeper becomes their sense of contrition. The after-perception of the enlightened mind views sin without illusion. Laodicea at last has her eyes open.

Nevertheless, this repentance is the opposite of despair or gloom. When we can view our sinful state with the repentance of enlightened "after perception," we can truly appreciate the "good news." Those who fear repentance lest it induce gloom or sadness misunderstand the mind of Christ and close their hearts to the healing power of the Holy Spirit. The laughter of the world is superficial and quickly turns to despair under trial. "Not as the world giveth" is the joy of Christ, consistent with His being a man of sorrows and acquainted with grief. As the remnant church ministers amidst the tragic disintegration of human life that will characterize the last days, that deep unfailing joy of the Lord will emerge from a realistic contrition.

Repentance for the individual is perceptive after-thought, a change of mind that views personal character in the light of Calvary. What was previously unrealized in the life becomes known. The deep-seated selfishness of the soul, the corruption of the motives, all are viewed in the light that streams from the cross.

Repentance for the church body is the same perceptive after-thought, but it views denominational history from the perspective of Calvary. What was previously unrealized within history becomes known. Movements and developments that were mysterious at the time are seen in their larger, truer significance. Pentecost forever defines this glorious reality of repentance.

The Why of Apostolic Success

The secret of the early church's success was an understanding that "ye crucified Christ," and then true repentance followed. Christ crucified became the central appeal of all the apostles' ministry. The Book of Acts would never have been written unless the members of the early church realized their share of the guilt of the murder of the Son of God, and likewise shared in the joyful experience of appropriate repentance.

From Acts 10 onwards we read of how others besides Jews partook of the same experience. The apostles marvelled that the Gentiles should experience the same phenomenal response to the cross that the believing Jews did, and thus receive the gift of the Holy Spirit (Acts 10:44-47).

The Holy Spirit sent their words closer home than they expected. Their contrite hearers identified themselves with the Jews and recognized their share of the guilt. In other words, the Gentiles experienced a corporate repentance.

Nothing in Scripture indicates that the full reception of the Holy Spirit in the last days will be any different.

Would You Have Done Better?

Let us picture ourselves in the crowd that gathered before Pilate that Friday morning. The strange Prisoner stands bound. It is popular to join in condemning Him. Not a voice is raised in His defense.

Suppose you are connected with Pilate's government, or are in the employ of Caiaphas, the High Priest. You support your family with your wages. Would you have the courage to stand up alone and say, "We are making a terrible mistake here! This man is not guilty of these charges. He is what He claims—He is the divine Son of God! I appeal to you, Pilate and Caiaphas, accept this Man as the Messiah!"

Suppose your own close circle of friends have already joined the mockery and abuse of Jesus; would you (or I) have the nerve to face them alone and rebuke them for what they do?

Realizing how easily a defense of Jesus might put you on the cross too, would you (or I) dare to speak out? Surely the answer is obvious.

We dare not say that the church as a world body cannot know this repentance, lest when we survey the wondrous cross on which the Prince of glory died, we pour contempt on his loving sacrifice by implying that it was in vain.

Chapter 10

What Our Denominational History Tells Us

Does our denominational history give meaning to Christ's call for last-day repentance? There are several possible ways of looking at our history:

(1) We can view our past with pride and satisfaction like a sports team that almost never loses a game. This attitude is thought to be loyalty, for it assumes that God's blessings on the church are His approval of our spiritual state. The result: pervasive lukewarmness. This is by far the most popular view of our history, but its spiritual pride is the opposite of New Testament faith which always includes the element of contrition.

(2) In contrast, others view our history with despair. There are real failures in our history which some interpret as evidence that the Lord has cast off this church. This view has produced various offshoots, and continually spawns new movements of fruitless, destructive criticism. Often these movements are initiated as a legitimate protest against spiritual pride or apostasy, although they seldom offer a practical solution to the problem. But there is something that both groups hold in common:

Both strenuously oppose denominational repentance. The first group oppose it on the grounds that it is unnecessary. Even the suggestion is regarded as impertinent, disloyal, as the ancient priests regarded Jeremiah's appeals for national repentance. The second group reject it on the grounds that it is impossible, since they assume that the Lord has withdrawn from the church both the privilege and the possibility of such repentance. There is a third view possible:

(3) We can view our history with a confidence born of contrition. This is the realistic approach. This church is the true "remnant" of prophecy which God has led. But our failure to honor our Lord as prophecy indicates must be done requires that we fall to our knees. The world has not yet truly heard the message, and His people have not as yet been prepared for the return of Christ. This view "rejoiceth in the truth." It does not seek to evade or suppress the obvious facts of denominational history that call for repentance and reformation. Nevertheless, realism highlights the future with hope. The joy of the Lord always accompanies repentance.

Attempts to Explain the Long Delay

Truth always gives ground for hope. But human pride, if uncorrected, will destroy hope and cause large numbers of sincere church members to lose their way. Denying or suppressing the truth produces frustrated despair. The reason is that the human conscience recognizes the reality of the passage of time, the pervading spiritual inertia, and the distressing world outlook. An evasion of reality and a disregard of Christ's call to repent will inevitably destroy the morale of thoughtful, informed church members all over the world. The loss to the church is incalculable.

We are forced to confess that the long delay has to be explained in some way. Something somewhere has to "give." Four possible solutions have been suggested:

(a) **Some say that the integrity of the church itself must "give."** That is, its hopes have been disappointed because its very existence, they say, has become illegitimate. It has forfeited the favor of God, they add, and no longer represents a valid movement of His leading. This view, of course, rejects corporate and denominational repentance as impossible. Ultimately, it logically assumes a holier-than-thou stance.

(b) **Some theologians say that fundamental doctrines of the church must "give."** The pioneers were theologically naive. In particular, the sanctuary doctrine that built the Advent Movement into a unique denomination is not scriptural. Again, this proposed solution is a fatal consequence of decades of impenitence.

(c) **Some propagandists suggest that our understanding of "the Spirit of Prophecy" must "give."** Ellen White did not en-joy, they say, the extent of divine inspiration that we have thought was the case. She was inspired only in the sense that other nineteenth century religious writers were inspired. Something must "give," and the carnal heart having long resented Ellen White's high Christlike standards, it would like to destroy her prophetic credibility. "We will not have this man to reign over us" was the cry of rebellious Israel concerning Jesus. Now we face the same revolt against "the testimony of Jesus." It is ridiculed as a nineteenth century hangover.

(d) **Some suggest that the second coming of Christ took place at Pentecost.** The descent of the Holy Spirit at Pentecost was the real second Advent, they say, and it has been going on ever since. The longer the great delay continues, the stronger will be the temptation to re-structure the doctrine of the second coming and abandon belief in a personal, literal, imminent return of Jesus.

Implicit in all the above lurks a virtual charge against God Himself. "My Lord delayeth His coming" is the reechoing theme. From the days of the pioneers, it is assumed, He has mocked the prayers of a sincere people who have stood loyal to His commandments and the faith of Jesus against the ridicule of other Christian churches and the world. He has disappointed His people, not only on October 22, 1844, but continually ever since. The question at issue is the faithfulness of God!

Christ's Solution to Our Impasse

If Christ's call to "the angel of the church of the Laodiceans" is understood as a call to denominational repentance, then we can reconsider the four proposed solutions above: (a) The integrity of the church remains intact as the true "remnant" of the Bible prophecies. (b) Our foundational doctrines remain valid, being thoroughly scriptural. (c) Ellen White endures criticism and attacks as a true, honest agent who exercised the prophetic gift of "the testimony of Jesus." (d) The descent of the Holy Spirit at Pentecost is not confused with the future personal, literal second coming of Christ. The Lord has not delayed His coming nor has He mocked the sincere prayers of His people since 1844. The pioneers were truly led of the Holy Spirit in their understanding of the prophecies, the second advent, and the sanctuary. What must "give," then, is only our corporate, sinful, Laodicean pride which has thwarted all of our Lord's attempts to bring healing, unity, and reformation.

The alternative is frightening. If our Lord has delayed His coming, He has deceived us and we cannot trust Him in future.

If we have delayed the Lord's return, then there is hope. Something can be done. Our impenitence can be healed.

Insisting that our Lord has delayed His coming virtually destroys the Advent hope; recognizing that we have delayed it can validate and confirm our hope.

"Just Like the Jews"

Our historical parallel with the ancient Jewish nation is striking. They were God's true denominated people, enjoying as much evidence of His favor as we. Their pride in their denominational structure and organization was shown by their attitude, "The temple of the Lord, The temple of the Lord, The temple of the Lord, are these" (Jeremiah 7:4). The "temple" to us is our worldwide organization, which is as much a source of pride to us as was the temple to the ancient Jews. The Lord did indeed establish and bless the ancient temple, but the Jews' refusal of national repentance nullified its significance:

> The same disobedience and failure which were seen in the Jewish church have characterized in a greater degree the people who have had this great light from Heaven in the last messages of warning. Shall we let the history of Israel be repeated in our experience? Shall we, like them, squander our opportunities and privileges until God shall permit oppression and persecution to come upon us? Will the work which might be performed in peace and comparative prosperity be left undone until it must be performed in days of darkness, under the pressure of trial and persecution?
>
> There is a terrible amount of guilt for which the church is responsible (*Testimonies*, Vol. 5, pp. 456, 457.)

Whatever that guilt may be, she is still the one object of the Lord's supreme regard. Without the atonement of Christ, it is devastating to any individual's self-respect to face the reality of his or her guilt. It is the same with the church body. In order to face this "terrible amount of guilt" without discouragement, we also must see how God's love for the church as a body is unchanging. Again, this involves recognizing the creative aspect of God's *agape* love. Critics who are ready to abandon hope for the church are unwittingly at war with the fundamental truth of God's character—"God is *agape*" (1 John 4:8). The "final atonement" that we have long talked about must include a final reconciliation with the reality of His divine character in the setting of the antitypical Day of Atonement. Where the Jews failed, the remnant church must overcome in response to grace which does "much more abound."

Many inspired statements liken our denominational failure to that of the Jews. A very few examples must suffice:

> Since the time of the Minneapolis [1888] meeting, I have seen the state of the Laodicean church as never before. I have heard the rebuke of God spoken to those who feel so well satisfied, who know not their spiritual destitution. ... Like the Jews, many have closed their eyes lest they should see (*Review and Herald*, August 26, 1890).

> There is less excuse in our day for stubbornness and unbelief than there was for the Jews in the days of Christ. ... Many say, "If I had only lived in the days of Christ, ... I would not have rejected and crucified Him, as did the Jews;" but that will be proved by the way in which you deal with His message and His messengers today. The Lord is testing His people of today as He tested the Jews in their day.

> If ... we travel over the same ground, cherish the same spirit, refuse to receive reproof and warning, then our guilt will be greatly augmented, and the condemnation that fell upon them will fall upon us (*Review and Herald*, April 11, 1893).

> All the universe of heaven witnessed the disgraceful treatment of Jesus Christ, represented by the Holy Spirit [at the 1888 Session]. Had Christ been before them, they ["our own brethren"] would have treated Him in a manner similar to that in which the Jews treated Christ. (*Special Testimonies*, Series A, No. 6, p. 20).

Men professing godliness have despised Christ in the person of His messengers [1888]. Like the Jews, they reject God's message (*Fundamentals of Christian Education*, p. 472).

As surely as the Jews' history illustrates their need for a national repentance, so does our 1888 history illustrate our need for repentance and a final atonement. The inspired messenger of the Lord was quick to see it. The 1888 Conference was a miniature Calvary, according to Ellen White, a demonstration of the same spirit of unbelief and opposition to God's righteousness that inspired the ancient Jews. The spirit that actuated the opposers of the message was not a minor misunderstanding, a temporary underestimate of a debatable doctrine. It was inward rebellion against the Lord. If the Lord's messenger means what she says over and over, it was a re-enactment of the crucifixion of Christ—in principle.

How Our History Discloses Enmity Against God

Bear in mind that these facts in no way diminish the truth that the Seventh-day Adventist church was then and is now the "remnant church." The brethren who opposed the 1888 message were the true "angel of the church of the Laodiceans," and God did not cast them off. Our history makes Christ's call to repent come alive, and the only reason it has not come alive sooner is that it has not been understood. The church is basically honest at heart, and the long delay in repentance is solely due to the truth having been misconstrued and distorted.

Whereas the ancient Jews rejected their long-awaited Messiah, we rejected our long-awaited outpouring of the Holy Spirit in the latter rain. Note some points of comparison:

(a) **The Jews' Messiah was born in a stable.** The beginning of the latter rain in 1888 was manifested in surprisingly humble circumstances. Both events caught the respective leaders by surprise.

(b) **The Jews failed to discern the Son of God in lowly guise.** We failed to discern in the humble and sometimes faulty message of 1888 the beginning of the eschatalogical opportunity of the ages.

(c) The Jews were afraid Jesus would destroy their denominational structure. We feared that the 1888 message would damage the uniqueness of the church and perhaps destroy its effectiveness through uplifting faith rather than the works of the law as the way of salvation.

(d) The opposition of Jewish leaders influenced many to reject Jesus. The persistent opposition of prominent leading brethren in the years that followed 1888 influenced many younger workers and laity either to disregard the message or to misunderstand it. The church at large would have accepted the message had it come to them unopposed by leadership*

(e) The Jewish nation never repented of their sin. Thus they never recovered the blessings that Jesus' lordship would have brought to them. We have never as a denomination faced our corporate guilt and repented of our rejection of the beginning of the outpouring of the Holy Spirit. For this reason we have never as yet enjoyed the full blessings of its renewal. The very obvious reality of a century of history demonstrates this truth.

Note how the gospel commission could have been finished nearly a century ago:

> The influence that grew out of the resistance of light and truth at Minneapolis tended to make of no effect the light God had given to His people through the Testimonies. ...
>
> If every soldier of Christ had done his duty, if every watchman on the walls of Zion had given the trumpet a certain sound, the world might ere this have heard the message of warning. But the work is years behind. What account will be rendered to God for thus retarding the work? (*General Conference Bulletin*, 1893, p. 419.)
>
> The light that is to lighten the whole earth with its glory was resisted, and by the action of our own brethren has been in a great degree kept away from the world (*Selected Messages*, Book One, p. 235).

This humble messenger believed to her end that the Seventh-day Adventist church is the true "remnant" of Bible prophecy, entrusted with God's last gospel message of mercy. And she was loyal to the church unto the end, believing that repentance is the only response we can make that will enable Heaven to renew the gift of the Holy Spirit for the accomplishment of the long delayed task of proclaiming the message to the world.

The Full Truth is Uplifting, Not Depressing

The full truth is always up-beat, positive, encouraging. A distorted view of Peter's sermon at Pentecost could label it as "negative" because it called for repentance; but Pentecostal power for witnessing followed Pentecostal repentance. A repeat of this glorious phenomenon awaits our repentance and reconciliation with the Lord.

God's love for the world demands that His message of good news go everywhere, with power. We know that it is not unfair of the Lord to withhold from us further showers of the latter rain until we understand and repent in the same way that the Lord required ancient Israel to understand and repent. It can be said of us in truth, "Great is the wrath of the Lord that is kindled against us, because our fathers have not hearkened unto the words of this book, to do according unto all which is written concerning us" (2 Kings 22:13). We can pray as did Ezra, "From the days of our fathers down to this present day our guilt has been very great" (Ezra 9:7, NEB).

The reason is that the sins of spiritual fathers get ingrained into us, aside from repentance. That is what happened to ancient Israel. And even though we were very few in number in 1888, the character of that impenitence has been propagated throughout the worldwide body today like a spreading virus. The disease must run its course until repentance can eradicate it. Until then, each new generation absorbs the same lukewarmness.

This is not the Augustinian doctrine of original sin. There is no genetic transmission of guilt. We recognize the reality of how sin has been propagated ever since Eden—"through the medium of influence, taking advantage of the action of mind on mind, ... reaching from mind to mind" (*Review and Herald*, April 16, 1901).

Daniel's Corporate Repentance

Our position closely parallels that of Israel in the days of Daniel. He could have argued before the Lord, "Some of us and some of our fathers were true, Lord; look how faithful I have been, also Shadrach, Meshach, and Abednego! We have practiced health reform. Remember how some of our 'fathers' as Jeremiah, Baruch, and others, stood nobly for the truth in times of apostasy. We are not all guilty, Lord!"

But how did Daniel pray? Notice his use of the corporate "we":

> All Israel have transgressed Thy law, even by departing, that they might not obey Thy voice. … For our sins, and for the iniquities of our fathers, Jerusalem and Thy people are become a reproach to all that are about us … I was … confessing my sin and the sin of my people Israel (Daniel 9:11, 16, 20).

The fact that we were not personally present in 1888 makes no more difference than that Daniel was not living in the days of his fathers. Christ, in His own flesh, has shown us how to experience a repentance for sins in which we have not thought we were personally involved. If He, the sinless One, repented in behalf of the sins of the whole world, surely we can repent in behalf of the sins of our fathers, whose spiritual children we are today! The essential truth that cries for recognition is that their sin is ours, because of the reality of the Biblical principle of corporate guilt.

We must take a brief look at an argument that has been assumed to contradict the need for denominational repentance.

Did the 1901 General Conference Cancel the 1888 Unbelief?

Some have assumed that the 1901 General Conference Session was the scene of an about-face, a reformation that undid the rejection of the 1888 message and cancelled its consequences. This view implies the parallel assumption that the latter rain and the loud cry have been progressing ever since. Large baptisms and financial and institutional growth are often cited as evidence, even though the Mormons and Jehovah's Witnesses can also cite phenomenal statistical growth.

It is true that the 1901 session did bring great blessings. But it is also clear that no deep spiritual reformation occurred. The lady with keen discernment wrote to a friend a few months after the 1901 Session:

> The result of the last General Conference [1901] has been the greatest, the most terrible sorrow of my life. No change was made. The spirit that should have been brought into the whole work as the result of the meeting, was not brought in because men did not receive the testimonies of the Spirit of God. As they went to their several fields of labor, they did not walk in the light that the Lord had flashed upon their pathway, but carried into their work the wrong principles that have been prevailing in the work at Battle Creek (Ellen White letter to Judge Jesse Arthur, Elmshaven, January 14, 1903).

In consequence of this impenitence, the finishing of God's work was delayed an indefinite time:

> We may have to remain here in this world because of insubordination many more years, as did the children of Israel, but for Christ's sake His people should not add sin to sin by charging God with the consequence of their own wrong course of action (Letter December 7, 1901; M-184, 1901.)

Even so, it was not too late then to engage in an experience of repentance. The Lord's messenger did not use the phrase "denominational repentance," but she expressed the principle. "All" needed to participate:

> But if all now would only see and confess and repent of their own course of action in departing from the truth of God, and following human devisings, then the Lord would pardon (*Ibid.*)

John the Baptist could have spent several lifetimes trying to encompass all the needs for reformation in his day. He preferred to lay "the axe ... unto the root of the trees" (Matthew 3:10).**

Would repenting of our rejection of the beginning of the latter rain lay the axe unto the root of our present spiritual problem? Yes, for that is indeed its root. But roots have a way of lying beneath the visible surface.

---

* See Ellen G. White, *Selected Messages*, Book One, pp. 234, 235; *Review and Herald*, March 11, 18, 1890.

** If we were to list all of the current manifold departures from God's plan, we would weary the reader and weary the angels, too. It would take a shelf of books bigger than the Encyclopedia Britannica for critics to detail all of our departures from the "blueprint" in our educational, medical, health reform, evangelistic, and administrative functions of church organization and practice. These have been talked about and written about for generations. The sighing and crying and hand-wringing are endless. And it's easy to say that "conversion" will take care of the problem—we've said that also for generations. The "axe" wielded by the true Christ is different from that of the false and counterfeit "Christ." The "dragon" who is "wroth with the woman" seldom puts on his dragon costume; he can even dress up to look like a "reformer" and slash away at all kinds of branches with great zeal, taking care to leave the actual "root."

Chapter 11

Bible Repentance:
Path to Christlike Love

If "God is love," love is power. The final manifestation of the Holy Spirit will be a demonstration by the church of that powerful love of God:

> It is the darkness of misapprehension of God that is enshrouding the world. Men are losing their knowledge of His character. It has been misunderstood and misinterpreted. At this time a message from God is to be proclaimed, a message illuminating in its influence and saving in its power. His character is to be made known. ...
>
> The last rays of merciful light, the last message of mercy to be given to the world, is a revelation of His character of love. The children of God are to manifest His glory. In their own life and character they are to reveal what the grace of God has done for them (*Christ's Object Lessons*, pp. 415, 416.)

We recognize that this is yet future. No one can point to a time in our history and say, "Here this blessing was received, and here these final prophecies were fulfilled."

Love, the Purifying, Consuming Fire in the Coal

Love as agape is not a namby-pamby, mushy sentimentalism. The same God is who is agape is also "a consuming fire" (Hebrews 12:29). That fire is death to selfishness, sensuality, love of the world, pride and arrogance. When that true love does impregnate the church as fire permeates the coal, she will become super-efficient in soul winning. Each congregation, "Jerusalem" to its local community, will be what Christ would be to that community were He there in the flesh. Cleansed by fire, the church will become an extension of Christ's power to redeem lost people.

The Holy Spirit at last can do His final work in the human heart. This is because members will receive the "mind of Christ."

> Miracles will be wrought, the sick will be healed, and signs and wonders will follow the believers. ... The rays of light penetrate everywhere, the truth is seen in its clearness, and the honest children of God sever the bands which have held them. ... A large number take their stand upon the Lord's side" (*The Great Controversy*, p. 612).

What could those "rays of light" be except the love of God seen in His people? One's mind staggers to try to imagine the joy that will flow like a river when the Lord's pure good news goes forth in glory and power. How many human hearts now in darkness will meet Christ and find in Him their soul's longing!

Too often our congregation is a comfortable, exclusive religious club, whereas the Lord declares that it is "an house of prayer for all people," including "sinners" we haven't thought much about.

Why does God send sunlight and rain on "the just and the unjust," even His enemies? The answer: His love is something that is not natural for us to have. If we could manipulate the bounties of nature, we might easily feel that our discriminating between good and bad people would be more efficient in persuading the bad to become good than God's way of showering blessings on both alike.

Many people are counted by the Lord as His, scattered all around us, whom now we consider hopeless. Yet they are just as much His as was Mary Magdalene, or the thief on the cross. The moment we try to be selective in our love, we forfeit connection with the Holy Spirit.

As the Pharisees and scribes murmured, so we are too easily scandalized because Christ "receiveth sinners" (Luke 15:1, 2). But the greater the evil of the sinner, the greater is God's glory in redeeming him:

> The divine Teacher bears with the erring through all their perversity. His love does not grow cold; His efforts to win them do not

cease. With outstretched arms He waits to welcome again and again the erring, the rebellious, and even the apostate. … Though all are precious in His sight, the rough, sullen, stubborn dispositions draw most heavily upon His sympathy and love; for He traces from cause to effect. The one who is most easily tempted, and is most inclined to err, is the special object of His solicitude (*Education*, p. 294.)

Repentance Lights the Fire in the Coal

Now, to be practical, how can we learn this kind of love?

By seeing Christ as He truly is. Perfectly sinless, nevertheless His repentance "in behalf of the sins of the world" taught Him how weak He was apart from strength from His Father. He knew He could fall. Born in the river that sweeps us into sin through the force of its undertow, He stood firm on the rock of faith in His Father, perfectly resisting that undertow, even when it appeared that He was forsaken. The Father sent His Son "in the likeness of sinful flesh." In very truth He is our "brother." He bore the guilt of "every sinner."

Zechariah describes this vision of Christ: "They shall look upon Me whom they have pierced." When we thus look upon Him with understanding, we shall realize a new sense of oneness with Him. We will feel toward Him a heart union that will cancel out the appeal of worldly allurement and self-concern. This will indeed be a miracle.

The point of Zechariah's prophecy is that corporate repentance felt for corporate guilt will trigger the reception and exercise of this overflowing love. The ability to feel for and to love every sinner was the only way that Christ's heavenly agape could be true to itself. Its expression was the direct result of His own experience in our flesh of corporate repentance. And He encourages us. We too are to learn to love even as He has loved us. Zechariah's prophecy indicates a last-day miracle of "grace." The atonement effected at the cross and applied from the heavenly sanctuary will produce a cleansing in God's believing people.

Righteousness by Faith and Repentance

Only a repentance such as this can make sense of the expression, "The Lord our righteousness." The one who feels that by nature he has at least some righteousness of his own will feel that he is to that extent better than someone else. Feeling so, Christ to him will be a stranger. And so, then, must the sinner likewise be a stranger to him.

It is natural to human nature for us to abhor the genuine truth of Christ's righteousness. We naturally resent the contrition implicit in seeing in Christ all our righteousness. We shrink from putting ourselves in the place of the alcoholic, the drug addict, the criminal, the prostitute, the rebel, the derelict. We so easily say in heart, "I could never sink to such a depth."

So long as we feel thus, we are powerless to speak as Jesus did an effective word to help. Love for souls is frozen. Restrained and selfishly directed, it ceases to be love. It's bad enough that we decline to enter the kingdom of heaven ourselves through letting the Holy Spirit melt down our deep-frozen hearts. But it's worse that we can actually shut up the kingdom, barring the way so that neither the contemporary Mary Magdalene or the thief on the cross can surmount our obstacles to get in.

Blessed would be the millstone to be hung around the necks of unloving saints, and blessed would be their drowning in the sea, said Jesus, rather than that they should face in the Judgment the results of a lifelong lovelessness. "It were better not to live than to exist day by day devoid of that love which Christ has enjoined upon His children" (*Counsels to Teachers*, p. 266).

According to Christ's call, it is time now for us to understand that the guilt of the whole world's sin, its frustrated enmity against God, its despair, its rebellion—all is "mine" apart from the grace of God; and if Christ were to withdraw from me that grace, I would embody the whole of its evil, for "in me, that is in my flesh, dwelleth no good thing" (Romans 7:18). Until we fully appreciate that truth, we cannot fully realize the imparted righteousness of Christ.

This is why the repentance Christ begs us to accept takes us back to Calvary. It is impossible to repent truly of minor sins without repenting of the major sin which underlies all other sin. The heavenly High Priest is not in the business of plucking fruit off of bad trees. He will lay His axe unto the root, or He will leave the "tree" alone. The underlying idea behind the message of Christ's righteousness is that I possess not a shred of righteousness of my own, and only when I see it can I discern the gift of His.

"According to your faith be it unto you," is the measure of our receptivity. By true repentance, we accept the gift of contrition and forgiveness for all sin of which we are potentially capable, not merely for the few sins which we think we have personally committed. Thus we receive from Christ potential righteousness equal to His own perfection, at present far beyond our capacity. But it is as real as the potential guilt we can realize in behalf of the sins of the world.

The Miracle-working Power of Repentance

Like the Lord Himself, the penitent "delighteth in mercy," and discovers his greatest pleasure in finding apparently hopeless material and helping these people become subjects of God's grace:

> Tell the poor desponding ones who have gone astray that they need not despair. Though they have erred, and have not been building a right character, God has joy to restore to them, even the joy of His salvation. He delights to take apparently hopeless material, those through whom Satan has worked, and make them the subjects of His grace. … Tell them there is healing, cleansing for every soul. There is a place for them at the Lord's table. (*Christ's Object Lessons*, p. 234).

Paul's doctrine must at last come into its own, that the seed sown nearly two thousand years ago may begin to bear the blessed fruit that the whole creation has groaned and travailed together in pain to see.

The Holy Spirit Is Working

The repentance Christ calls for is already beginning to be realized. When one member in a congregation falls into sin, a little reflection can convince many of the members that they share in his or her guilt. Had we been more alert, more kind-hearted, more ready to speak "a word in season to him that is weary," more effective in communicating the pure, powerful truth of the gospel, we might have saved the erring member. With knowledgeable pastoral care, almost any church can at present be led to feel at least some of this corporate concern.

It is encouraging therefore to believe that within this generation, a large sense of loving concern can be realized on a worldwide scale. When this time comes (and it will come unless hindered), there will be a heart-unity and concern between races, nationalities, and social and economic cultures seldom seen as yet. The fulfillment of Christ's ideal will be on all levels and among all groups. The winter of frozen inhibitions and fears will give way to a glorious spring and summer where the loves and sympathies that God has implanted in our souls will find more true and pure expression to one another.

It will be impossible any longer to feel superior or patronizing toward people whose race, nationality, or culture is different from ours. With "the mind of Christ," a bond of sympathy and fellowship is established "in Him." This miracle will follow the laws of grace.

This will take God's people a step further. Instead of limiting itself to a shared repentance in behalf of our contemporary generation of the living, it will take in past generations as well. Paul's idea, "As the body is one, and hath many members, ... so also is Christ," will be seen to include the past body of Christ also. Thus Moses' command to repent for the sins of previous generations will make sense (Leviticus 26:40). The "final atonement" becomes a reality, and the pre-Advent judgment can then be concluded.

While there will be a shaking, and some, perhaps many, who refuse repentance will abandon fellowship, the inspired word implies that a true remnant of believers in Christ will remain. The shaking of the tree or branches is not all bad news. It offers the good news that "gleaning grapes shall be left in it" (cf. Isaiah 17:6; 24:13, emphasis added). Those who are left "shall lift up their voice, they shall sing for the majesty of the Lord" (verse 14). Those who are shaken out will only make "manifest that they were not all of us" (1 John 2:19). God's work will go forward unhindered and greatly strengthened.

In this time, the church will be united and coordinated like a healthy human body. Backbiting, evil-surmising, gossip, even forgetfulness of the needs of others, will be overcome. The listening ear, tuned to be sensitive to the call of the Holy Spirit, will hear and act upon the conviction of duty. When He says as He said to Philip the deacon, "Go near, and join thyself to this chariot," the obedient response will be immediate; and a soul will be won as Philip won the Ethiopian official from Can-dace's royal court. At last the Holy Spirit will find a perfectly responsive "temple" in which to dwell; and rejoicing over His people with singing, the Lord will gladly bring into their fellowship all His people now scattered in Babylon.

Miracles of heart-healing will come as if Christ Himself were present in the flesh. Chasms of estrangement will be bridged. Marital dissensions will find solutions that have evaded the best efforts of counselors and psychiatrists. Broken homes will be cemented in the bonds of love that elicits ultimate contrition from believing hearts. Harps now silent will ring with melody when the strings are touched by this hand. Bewildered and frustrated youth will see a revelation of Christ never before discerned. Satan's enchantment of drugs, liquor, immorality, and rebellion will lose its hold, and the pure, joyous tide of youthful devotion to Christ will flow to the praise of His grace. "The Lord shall arise upon thee, and his glory shall be seen upon thee. And the Gentiles shall come to thy light, and kings to the brightness of thy rising" (Isaiah 60:2, 3).

The world and the vast universe beyond will watch with wonder the final demonstration of the fruits of Christ's sacrifice. In a profound sense hardly dreamed of by the pioneers of the Advent Movement, the heavenly sanctuary, nerve center of God's great controversy with Satan, will be "cleansed," justified, set right before the universe.

The Church a Powerhouse of Ministering Love

Such an experience of repentance will transform the church into a dynamo of love. It is God's plan that no church will have seating capacity for the converted sinners who will stream into it. Because He took the steps the sinner must take in repentance, Christ was enabled to pass by no human being as "worthless." Corporate and denominational repentance is the whole church experiencing this same Christ-like love and empathy for all for whom He died.

Beware of the sinful unbelief that doubts how good the Good News is. Those who say, "It's too good to be true! It just can't happen!" should repent of rejecting the heavenly vision. In the days of Elisha, Samaria suffered a terrible siege famine. "A donkey's head cost eighty pieces of silver, and half a pound of dove's dung cost five pieces of silver." There was frightful cannibalism. Blaming the Lord for it all, the king wanted to kill the prophet. (Here was enmity against God in action!)

Elisha responded by promising that within twenty-four hours "ten pounds of the best wheat or twenty pounds of barley" would be selling in the city gates for only "one piece of silver." The instant reaction of "the personal attendant of the king" was unbelief—such plenty would be too good to be true. "That can't happen," he retorted,—not even if the Lord himself were to send grain at once!"

"You will see it happen, but you won't get any of the food," Elisha replied.

The story continues: "It so happened that the king of Israel had put the city gate under the command of the officer who was his personal attendant." The Lord frightened away the invading Syrians and they left their huge supplies for the starving Israelites. The officer was "trampled to death by the people at the city gate." (See 2 Kings 7:1-20, TEV).

Unbelief in this "time of the latter rain" will shut us out from taking part in the glorious experience that the Lord foretells for His people once they repent in response to His call. Inspired statements confirm the vision of the "whole church" within history fully experiencing such blessing, doubtless following its purification:

> The Holy Spirit is to animate and pervade the whole church, purifying and cementing hearts (*Testimonies*, Vol 9, p. 20).

> The time has come for a thorough reformation to take place. When this reformation begins, the spirit of prayer will actuate every

believer, and will banish from the church the spirit of discord and strife. ... All will be in harmony with the mind of God (*Ibid.*, Vol. 8, p. 251).

In visions of the night representations passed before me of a great reformatory movement among God's people. ... A spirit of intercession was seen, even as was manifested before the great day of Pentecost. ... Hearts were convicted by the power of the Holy Spirit, and a spirit of genuine conversion was manifest. On every side doors were thrown open to the proclamation of the truth. The world seemed to be lightened with the heavenly influence. ... There seemed to be a reformation such as we witnessed in 1844.

Yet some refused to be converted. ... These covetous ones became separated from the company of believers (*Ibid.*, Vol. 9, p. 126).

Here is where we take off our shoes for we tread solemnly on holy ground. This modest volume has attempted to explore Christ's call to the angel of His church to repent. Let us pray that the Spirit of God may employ many voices to echo the call. Let no one underestimate the importance of his or her personal, individual response. Perhaps all the Lord needs is to find *one* person somewhere who is baptized and crucified and risen "with Christ" and who thus shares *His* experience of repentance.

Then the precious leaven of truth can permeate the whole body.

Appendix A

A Repentance of Ministers
And Their Families

The following statement from Ellen White indicates the depth of response that will come from ministers and their wives and children:

In the night season I was in my dreams in a large meeting, with ministers, their wives, and their children. I wondered that the company present was mostly made up of ministers and their families. The prophecy of Malachi was brought before them in connection with Daniel, Zephaniah, Haggai, and Zechariah. ... There was close searching of the Scriptures in regard to the sacred character of all that appertained to the temple service. ...

After a diligent searching of the Scriptures, there was a period of silence. A very solemn impression was made upon the people. The deep moving of the Spirit of God was manifest among us. All were troubled, all seemed to be convicted, burdened, and distressed, and they saw their own life and character represented in the word of God, and the Holy Spirit was making the application to their hearts.

Conscience was aroused. The record of past days was making its disclosure of the vanity of human inventions. The Holy Spirit brought all things to their remembrance. As they reviewed their past history, there were revealed defects of character that ought to have been discerned and corrected. They saw how through the grace of Christ the character should have been transformed. The workers had known the sorrow of defeat in the work intrusted to their hands, when they should have had victory.

The Holy Spirit presented before them Him whom they had offended. They saw that God will not only reveal himself as a God of mercy and forgiveness and long forbearance, but by terrible things in righteousness He will make it manifest that He is not a man that He should lie.

Words were spoken by One, saying, "The hidden, inner life will be revealed. As if reflected in a mirror, all the inward working of the character will be made manifest. The Lord would have you examine your own lives, and see how vain is human glory.'Deep calleth unto deep at the noise of thy waterspouts; all thy waves and thy billows are gone over me. Yet the Lord will command His loving-kindness in the daytime, and in the night His song shall be with me, and my prayer unto the God of my life." (*Review and Herald*, February 4, 1902).

Appendix B

Laodicea Is Not Doomed

Serious efforts have been made to convince church members to leave the organized Seventh-day Adventist Church, or at least to withdraw their support and fellowship. The argument is that Philadelphia, not Laodicea, represents the true church that will get ready for Christ's coming. Joseph Bates is cited as a venerable authority for this view. But this dear pioneer was mistaken in this, as he was on some other points as well. Ellen White never lent her endorsement to this idea of his. Her early testimonies about the Laodicean message thoroughly contradict his view (see *Testimonies*, Vol. 1, pp. 185-195; *Testimonies*, Vol. 3, pp. 252-255).

The idea that Philadelphia, not Laodicea, is the translation church conflicts with the general pattern of the prophetic picture in Revelation. The number seven indicates that the seven churches symbolize the true church through succeeding periods of history from the time of the apostles to the close of probation (*Acts of the Apostles*, pp. 581, 583, 585). The message to Laodicea is "the warning for the last church," not the next-to-the-last one (*Testimonies*, Vol. 6, p. 77). The message does not apply to apostates, but to God's true people in the last days (*Bible Commentary*, Vol 7, p. 959; *Testimonies*, Vol. 3, pp. 252, 253).

The Lord's intention has always been that the message to Laodicea result in repentance and overcoming on the part of His true people and that it prepare them to receive the latter rain (*Testimonies*, Vol. 1, pp. 186, 187). There is no hint in Scripture or the Spirit of Prophecy that the message will ultimately fail; God's true people will heed "the counsel of the True Witness, and they will receive the latter rain, and thus be fitted for translation" (pp. 187, 188). Nowhere does Ellen White say that God's true people must leave Laodicea and return to Philadelphia.

It is, of course, true that spiritual applications can be made from *all* of the messages to the seven churches, appropriate to God's people in all generations. Human nature is the same the world over and in all generations, so that spiritual principles apply to all. But the messages to the seven churches reveal a progression of victorious overcoming that will enable the last generation finally to reach a maturity of faith and understanding. "The harvest of the earth" will at last be "ripe" (Revelation 14:12-15). Heart acceptance of truths in all the appeals to "the angels of the seven churches" will be necessary for this eventual ripening of the "full corn in the ear ... when the fruit is brought forth" (Mark 4:28, 29). But for the last-day church to return to Philadelphia would be to set the clock back to a previous generation and violate the prophetic symbolism. The messages to the six churches have prepared multitudes of believers for death; repentance on the part of Laodicea prepares a people for translation.

The message to Laodicea parallels the time of the cleansing of the sanctuary and the work of Christ in the Most Holy Apartment. The obvious intent of the Revelation symbolism is to relate Laodicea with the time of the "seventh angel" sounding his trumpet during the "time of the dead, that they should be judged" when "the temple of God was opened in heaven" and the Most Holy Apartment came to view (Revelation 11:15-19).

The message to Philadelphia obviously *precedes* the antitypical Day of Atonement, fittingly parallel to the "mighty angel's" work of Revelation 10, which also precedes the final message of the three angels (vs. 11). To change the order of the seven churches is as confusing as changing the order of the seven seals or the seven trumpets. God knew what He was about when He gave the visions to John at Patmos, and we dare not tamper with the inspired order of these messages.

Quotations from the message to Philadelphia which Ellen White applies to people in the last days do not require that Laodicea be eliminated from the prophetic succession, any more than her frequent quotations from others of the seven messages require that we "join" Ephesus, Smyrna, Pergamos, Thyatira, or Sardis.

The problem with Laodicea is not with its identity or with its name. Laodicea is not a dirty word—it simply means "judging, vindicating, or justifying, the people." It is a name appropriate to the realities of the investigative judgment that precedes the second coming. It connotes victory, not defeat.

The name Philadelphia is also significant. It is compounded from *phileo*, meaning affection, and *adelphos*, brother. The word *phileo* denotes a lower level of love than *agape*. But "speaking the truth in *agape*" and growing "up into Him in all things, which is the head, even Christ" is the experience that will characterize God's people as they grow in maturity in preparation for Christ's coming. "The whole body" of the church, the corporate whole of God's people of all ages, will at last make "increase of the body unto the edifying [building up] of itself in *agape*" (cf. Ephesians 3:14-19; 4:13-16; *Early Writings*, pp. 55, 56; *Christ's Object Lessons*, pp. 415, 416).

As noted elsewhere in this book, the expression "I will spue thee out of my mouth" is not an accurate translation of the Greek. Christ did not say that Laodicea must suffer His final rejection, without hope. The Greek is *mello se emesai*, which means literally, "You make Me sick with nausea," or "I am so nauseated that I am on the point of vomiting." But the verb *mello* does not require a final action. Christ's nausea can be healed; it is possible for Laodicea to repent and thus to overcome her terrible lukewarmness.

Read Christ's letters to the angels of the seven churches at one sitting, consecutively. It will be very evident that they show an historical goal direction oriented toward the return of Christ. Thyatira is pointed forward "till I come." Sardis is pointed forward to the pre-advent judgment. Philadelphia is told, "I come quickly." But Laodicea meets Christ "at the door," and is offered the ultimate honor of sharing with Him His royal authority.

Another internal evidence that Laodicea is the last church is Christ's introduction of Himself as "the Amen." This is a word that throughout the New Testament expresses finality.

Christ's message to Laodicea is closely related to the Song of Solomon 5:2, which He quotes (from the LXX version) in Revelation 3:20. This often neglected truth establishes Christ's Laodicean appeal as that of the Bridegroom to His beloved. Her eventual response is not rejection of the Bridegroom's love, but repentance and preparation for the "marriage of the Lamb" (Revelation 19:6-9). Thus the promise to the "certain one" of Revelation 3:21 (Greek, *tis*) is the offer of an intimacy in relationship to Christ that is not matched in any of the offers to the previous six "angels of the seven churches." "The angel" of the last church is clearly the one whose repentance is unique, and whose overcoming at last presupposes a unique victory and unique honor—that of sharing executive authority with Christ Himself. A higher destiny awaits the Bride than those who are merely "guests" at the wedding. It is difficult not to recognize the relationship between Revelation 3:21 and the glorious victory of the 144,000 (7:1-4; 14:1-5; 15:2-4).

Thus it becomes clear that to cancel Laodicea out of the prophetic picture, to consider the True Witness's appeal to end in failure, is to rob Christ of the honor and vindication He so richly deserves. It violates the fulfillment of the prophecies in Revelation. Cancelling Laodicea and substituting Philadelphia requires the defeat of the True Witness, and the final humiliation of the patient Bridegroom who is still knocking at the door.

Appendix C

Ezekiel 18 and Corporate Guilt

Does Ezekiel deny the principle of corporate guilt? He says:

> What mean ye, that ye use this proverb, ... The fathers have eaten sour grapes, and the children's teeth are set on edge. ... Behold, all souls are Mine; as the soul of the father, so also the soul of the son is Mine: the soul that sinneth, it shall die. ...
>
> The son shall not bear the iniquity of the father, neither shall the father bear the iniquity of the son: the righteousness of the righteous shall be upon him, and the wickedness of the wicked shall be upon him. (Ezekiel 18:2, 4, 20; cf. Jeremiah 31:29, 30).

Ezekiel discusses a good man who does everything right, but who has a son who does everything wrong. Then he discusses how the wicked man's son "seeth all his father's sins ... and doeth not such like ... He shall not die for the iniquity of his father" (verses 14-17). Sin and guilt are not passed on genetically. The prophet's point is to recognize the principle of personal responsibility. The son need not repeat his father's sins unless he chooses to. He can break the cycle of corporate guilt by means of repentance.

But Ezekiel does not suggest that any righteous man is righteous of himself, nor does he deny the Bible truth of justification by faith. Any righteous man must be righteous by faith; apart from Christ he has no righteousness of his own. The wicked man is the one who rejects such righteousness by faith. The prophet does not deny that "all have sinned," and "all the world ... [is] guilty before God" (Romans 3:23, 19). Apart from the imputed righteousness of Christ, therefore, all the world is alike guilty before God.

The son who saw his father's sins and repented is delivered from the guilt of those sins by virtue of Christ's righteousness imputed to him, but he is not intrinsically better than his father. There is a sense in which the son's repentance is a corporate one: he realizes that had he been in his father's place he could have been just as guilty. He does not think he could not do such sins. He humbly confesses, "There but for the grace of God am I." Now he chooses the path of righteousness. Ezekiel is not denying the truth of corporate repentance; he upholds it.

www.ingramcontent.com/pod-product-compliance
Lightning Source LLC
Chambersburg PA
CBHW020322130626
46549CB00003B/977